25 Essential Projects
for Your

BEST OF POPULAR WOODWORKING MAGAZINE

Workshop

POPULAR
WOODWORKING
BOOKS

CINCINNATI, OHIO
www.popularwoodworking.com

READ THIS IMPORTANT SAFETY NOTICE

To prevent accidents, keep safety in mind while you work. Use the safety guards installed on power equipment; they are for your protection. When working on power equipment, keep fingers away from saw blades, wear safety goggles to prevent injuries from flying wood chips and sawdust, wear headphones to protect your hearing and consider installing a dust vacuum to reduce the amount of airborne sawdust in your woodshop. Don't wear loose clothing, such as neckties or shirts with loose sleeves, or jewelry, such as rings, necklaces or bracelets, when working on power equipment. Tie back long hair to prevent it from getting caught in your equipment. People who are sensitive to certain chemicals should check the chemical content of any product before using it. The authors and editors who compiled this book have tried to make the contents as accurate and correct as possible. Plans, illustrations, photographs and text have been carefully checked. All instructions, plans and projects should be carefully read, studied and understood before beginning construction. Due to the variability of local conditions, construction materials, skill levels, etc., neither the authors nor Popular Woodworking Books assume any responsibility for any accidents, injuries, damages or other losses incurred resulting from the material presented in this book.

METRIC CONVERSION CHART

TO CONVERT	TO	MULTIPLY BY
Inches	Centimeters	2.54
Centimeters	Inches	0.4
Feet	Centimeters	30.5
Centimeters	Feet	0.03
Yards	Meters	0.9
Meters	Yards	1.1
Sq. Inches	Sq. Centimeters	6.45
Sq. Centimeters	Sq. Inches	0.16
Sq. Feet	Sq. Meters	0.09
Sq. Meters	Sq. Feet	10.8
Sq. Yards	Sq. Meters	0.8
Sq. Meters	Sq. Yards	1.2
Pounds	Kilograms	0.45
Kilograms	Pounds	2.2
Ounces	Grams	28.4
Grams	Ounces	0.04

25 Essential Projects for Your Workshop. Copyright © 2000 by Popular Woodworking Books. Manufactured in China. All rights reserved. No part of this book may be reproduced in any form or by any electronic or mechanical means including information storage and retrieval systems without permission in writing from the publisher, except by a reviewer, who may quote brief passages in a review. Published by Popular Woodworking Books, an imprint of F&W Publications, Inc., 1507 Dana Avenue, Cincinnati, Ohio, 45207. First edition.

Visit our Web site at www.popularwoodworking.com for information on more resources for woodworkers.

Other fine Popular Woodworking Books are available from your local bookstore or direct from the publisher.

04   03   02   01   00   5   4   3   2   1

Library of Congress Cataloging-in-Publication Data

25 Essential Projects for Your Workshop / Best of Popular Woodworking magazine.
    p. cm.
    title: Twenty-five essential projects for your workshop
    Includes index.
    ISBN 1-55870-541-4 (alk. paper)
    1. Woodworking tools. 2. Woodwork--Equipment and supplies--Design and construction. 3. Workshops--Equipment and supplies--Design and construction. I. Popular Woodworking Books (Firm)
TT186 .A18 2000
684'.08--dc21

99-462302

Edited by Michael Berger and Jennifer Churchill
Content edited by Mark Thompson
Designed by Brian Roeth
Interior Production by Donna Cozatchy
Production coordinated by Sara Dumford

CREDITS

Staff of *Popular Woodworking* magazine

Christopher Schwarz, Senior Editor: *Project 3*/Benjamin Seaton's Tool Chest; *Project 10*/Stanley Tool Cabinet; *Project 16*/Hand Screws
Steve Shanesy, Editor & Publisher: *Project 1*/The Little Shop That Could
Jim Stuard, Associate Editor: *Project 2*/Little Shop Mark II; *Project 4*/Bullet-proof Bench; *Project 6*/Shop Stool; *Project 11*/Table Saw Organizer; *Project 12*/Lathe Tool Cabinet; *Project 17*/Sharpening Kit
David Thiel, Senior Editor: *Project 5*/Practical Router Table; *Project 7*/Adjustable Sawhorse; *Project 8*/Drill Press Table; *Project 13*/Wall-Mounted Clamp Rack; *Project 14*/Rolling Clamp Rack; *Project 20*/Table Saw Miter Sled; *Project 21*/Sandpaper Press

Contributors

R.J. DeCristoforo: *Project 22*/Band Saw Master Jig (excerpted from "The Ultimate Woodshop Jig Book" by R.J. DeCristoforo; copyright © 1999, Popular Woodworking Books)
Nick Engler: *Project 18*/Tilting Router Stand
Glen Huey: *Project 19*/Table Saw Tenon Jig
Troy Sexton: *Project 23*/Dovetail Jig
Michel Theriault: *Project 15*/Stacking Storage Boxes
Angelo Varisco: *Project 25*/Circle-cutting Jig

Introduction

When this book was first discussed, a lot of titles were considered and loudly debated. No fistfights, but it was close. Everyone had a different idea of what this book was all about, and nailing down a title that satisfied all those opinions was a struggle.

The problem is that a workshop is a very personal thing, even when it's a shared one like ours. Your workshop is a refuge from the real world, a peaceful haven from life's demands, even with the tools at full song. Shops are like fingerprints or favorite foods. What you like in your shop may be totally foreign to what we prefer, and vice versa.

There's simply no one-size-fits-all to workshops or the fixtures and equipment that go into them. Your choices of tools and how they're arranged say as much about your personality as the clothes you wear or the car you drive. You may be a flannel-shirt guy in your shop choices, while we're the polyester-leisure-suit types.

So What's In Here?

This book will show you how to build over 30 fixtures, jigs, helpers and storage solutions. Many of these projects began as a part of *Popular Woodworking* magazine. We know these projects intimately because we use everything in here on a regular basis. None of that dream-shop stuff. These are real projects for real people.

You'll find complete information and building plans. There's nothing so complex that you'd need gobs of new tools (sorry about that) or decades of woodworking experience. These are just good, all-around projects for real-world woodshops.

Because we spend so much time knee-deep in sawdust, we're always looking for ways to make our shared workshop more comfortable, the tools more versatile and storage more convenient. We've developed jigs and shop solutions for various common situations, and many of those creations have made it into the pages of *Popular Woodworking* magazine over the years. This is the first time they've been collected in one place, all for your benefit.

Many of our best project ideas actually come from our readers. The "Little Shop That Could," our $500 small-space workshop, came about that way. Challenged by our readers to devise a way to get maximum woodworking bang for minimum bucks, the Little Shop was our answer. From the first time this project article was published, it was a runaway reader favorite that sold out the issue and led us to offer reprints, which also sold out. Now, for the first time, it's available in a book, along with its big brother, the Little Shop Mark II — a larger, better-equipped mobile workstation that incorporates a number of improvements we discovered while living with the Little Shop.

Now, traditionally, workshop books are generic beasts, trying to find solutions for everyone by showing lots of examples. Unfortunately, most of those books don't deliver much practical information that you can use in your workshop ... right now, today.

Not so here. We're a project-oriented magazine and so is this book. Everything shown here has been built, improved, fine-tuned and otherwise forced to evolve. They've got the scars to prove it. Everything in this book sees regular use in our woodshop, and if we can build it, so can you.

This entire book is full of ways to make your workshop better, more useful, more enjoyable — which is how we approach all of our projects.

Enjoy!

The Editors

Log onto www.popularwoodworking.com for a look at our latest issue.

Much better-looking in person, PopWood staff members are (front row) Amy Schneider, Jim Stack, Brian Roeth, Mike Berger; (back row) Steve Shanesy, Mark Thompson, Jim Stuard. Missing faces: Jennifer Churchill, Chris Schwarz and David Thiel.

PHOTO BY CHRISTINE POLOMSKY

Table of Contents

PROJECTS

TIPS AND CHARTS

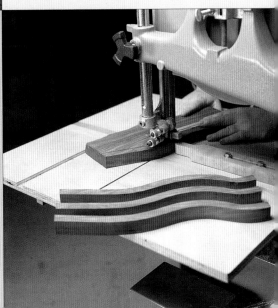

The Little Shop That Could

You say your shop space is too limited? You don't have enough tools (as if anyone does)? You dream about building this or that project if only ... if only you could win the lottery and build a climate-controlled pole barn that has more machinery and equipment than a dealer's showroom floor? You betcha. But, hey, keep your daydreams, just don't let those fantasies keep you from enjoying your craft today.

I've heard many readers say they share shop space with a car or a washer and dryer, so I concluded it would be appropriate for us at your favorite woodworking magazine to set up shop as many of you do — with limited space and an equally limited budget. I challenged myself to put together a shop with no more than $500 to spend on tools and equipment. The shop had to be mobile and self-contained — and it had to be small enough to be pushed up against the garage wall so the car could fit, or to be stored out of the way under the basement stairs.

Given these limitations, the shop would still have to be easy to set up, convenient to work in, and able to produce quality projects. After spending an hour researching prices at one of the big home-center stores, I was nearly convinced that with more diligent shopping, I could meet the $500 part of the challenge. A couple more hours of doodling with a pencil and paper gave me plans for a mobile, folding work center. Part two of the challenge was solved. Lastly, I decided that to produce quality projects with my limited equipment, I'd have to rely on a few shop-made jigs and a lot of creative problem-solving.

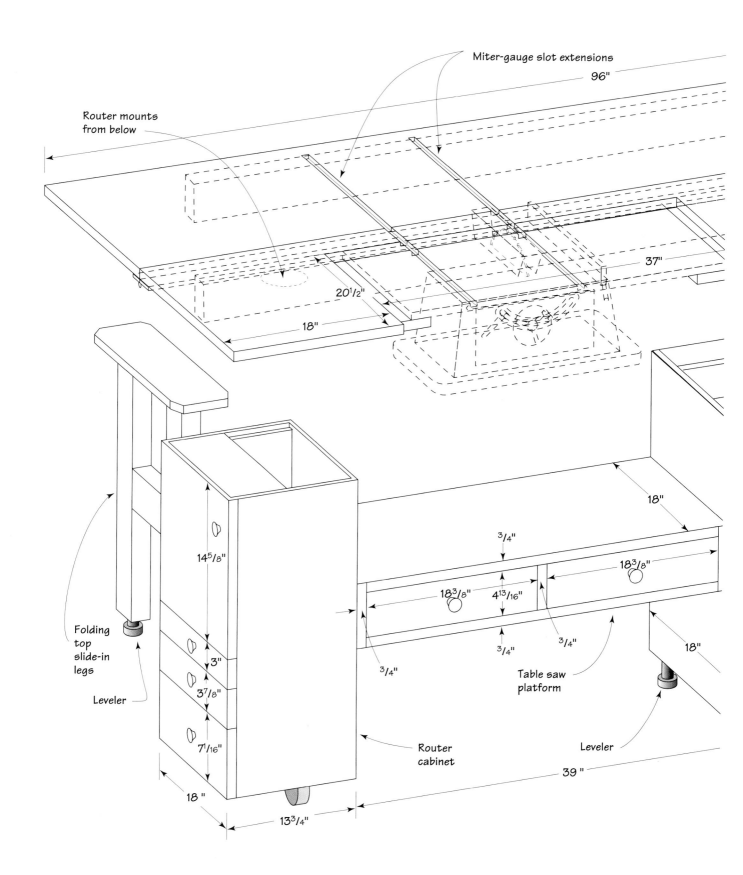

Miter-gauge slot extensions

96"

Router mounts from below

37"

20¹/₂"

18"

Folding top slide-in legs

Leveler

14⁵/₈"

3"

3⁷/₈"

7¹/₁₆"

18 "

13³/₄"

³/₄"

18³/₈"

4¹³/₁₆"

³/₄"

18³/₈"

³/₄"

18"

18"

Router cabinet

Table saw platform

Leveler

39 "

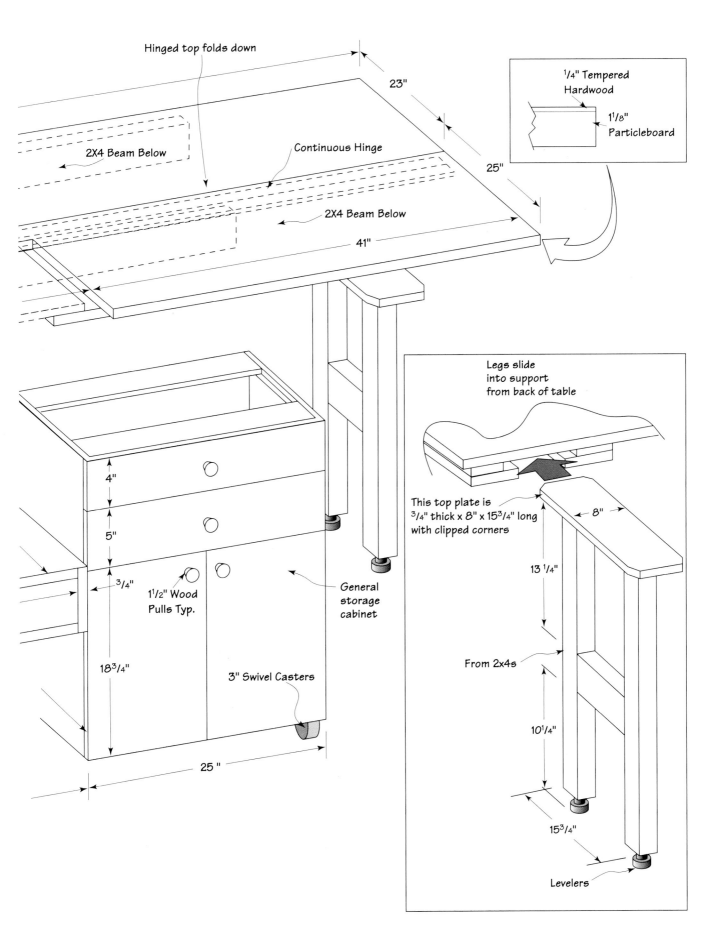

Hinged top folds down

23"

1/4" Tempered Hardwood

1 1/8" Particleboard

2X4 Beam Below

Continuous Hinge

25"

2X4 Beam Below

41"

Legs slide into support from back of table

4"

5"

This top plate is 3/4" thick x 8" x 15 3/4" long with clipped corners

8"

3/4"

1 1/2" Wood Pulls Typ.

General storage cabinet

13 1/4"

From 2x4s

18 3/4"

3" Swivel Casters

10 1/4"

25 "

15 3/4"

Levelers

9

Schedule of Materials • Router Cabinet

No.	Item	Dimensions T W L
2	Sides	$\frac{3}{4}$" x 13" x 29"
1	Back	$\frac{3}{4}$" x 17$\frac{1}{2}$" x 28$\frac{3}{4}$"
1	Bottom	$\frac{3}{4}$" x 13" x 17$\frac{1}{2}$"
1	Top stretcher (front)	$\frac{3}{4}$" x 4" x 17$\frac{1}{2}$"
1	Door	$\frac{3}{4}$" x 18" x 14$\frac{5}{8}$"
1	Drawer front	$\frac{3}{4}$" x 18" x 3"
1	Drawer subfront	$\frac{1}{2}$" x 2$\frac{1}{2}$" x 15$\frac{11}{16}$" + $\frac{1}{2}$"
1	Drawer back	$\frac{1}{2}$" x 2" x 15$\frac{11}{16}$" + $\frac{1}{2}$"
2	Drawer sides	$\frac{1}{2}$" x 2$\frac{1}{2}$" x 12"
1	Drawer bottom	$\frac{1}{4}$" x 11$\frac{3}{4}$" x 15$\frac{1}{2}$" + $\frac{1}{2}$"
1	Drawer front	$\frac{3}{4}$" x 18" x 3$\frac{7}{8}$"
1	Drawer subfront	$\frac{1}{2}$" x 2$\frac{3}{4}$" x 15$\frac{1}{4}$"
1	Drawer back	$\frac{1}{2}$" x 2$\frac{1}{4}$" x 15$\frac{1}{4}$"
2	Drawer sides	$\frac{1}{2}$" x 2$\frac{3}{4}$" x 12"
1	Drawer bottom	$\frac{1}{4}$" x 11$\frac{3}{4}$" x 15"
1	Drawer front	$\frac{3}{4}$" x 18" x 7"
1	Drawer subfront	$\frac{1}{2}$" x 5$\frac{1}{2}$" x 15$\frac{1}{4}$"
1	Drawer back	$\frac{1}{2}$" x 5" x 15$\frac{1}{4}$"
1	Drawer side	$\frac{1}{2}$" x 5$\frac{1}{2}$" x 12"
1	Drawer bottom	$\frac{1}{4}$" x 11$\frac{3}{4}$" x 15"

Schedule of Materials • Table Saw Platform

No.	Item	Dimensions T W L
2	Sides*	$\frac{3}{4}$" x 5" x 18"
2	Top & bottom*	$\frac{3}{4}$" x 18" x 39"
1	Back*	$\frac{3}{4}$" x 5" x 37$\frac{1}{2}$"
1	Partition*	$\frac{3}{4}$" x 5" x 17$\frac{1}{4}$"

* All butt joints glued and screwed. Top and bottom overlay sides, back, partition.

2	Drawer fronts	$\frac{3}{4}$" x 4$\frac{7}{8}$" x 18$\frac{5}{16}$"
2	Drawer subfronts	$\frac{1}{2}$" x 4" x 17$\frac{3}{16}$"
2	Drawer backs	$\frac{1}{2}$" x 3$\frac{1}{2}$" x 17$\frac{3}{16}$"
4	Drawer sides	$\frac{1}{2}$" x 4" x 16"
2	Drawer bottoms	$\frac{1}{4}$" x 15$\frac{3}{4}$" x 16$\frac{7}{8}$"

Schedule of Materials • General Storage Cabinet

No.	Item	Dimensions T W L
2	Sides	$\frac{3}{4}$" x 17$\frac{3}{16}$" x 29"
1	Back	$\frac{3}{4}$" x 24$\frac{1}{2}$" x 28$\frac{1}{2}$"
1	Bottom	$\frac{3}{4}$" x 17$\frac{3}{16}$" x 24$\frac{1}{2}$"
2	Stretchers	$\frac{3}{4}$" x 4" x 24$\frac{1}{2}$"
1	Rail	$\frac{3}{4}$" x 4" x 24$\frac{1}{4}$"
1	Drawer front	$\frac{3}{4}$" x 25" x 4"
1	Drawer subfront	$\frac{1}{2}$" x 3" x 22$\frac{5}{16}$"
1	Drawer back	$\frac{1}{2}$" x 2$\frac{1}{2}$" x 22$\frac{5}{16}$"
2	Drawer sides	$\frac{1}{2}$" x 3" x 16"
2	Drawer bottoms	$\frac{1}{4}$" x 15$\frac{3}{4}$" x 22"
1	Drawer front	$\frac{3}{4}$" x 25" x 5$\frac{3}{4}$"
1	Drawer subfront	$\frac{1}{2}$" x 4$\frac{1}{2}$" x 22$\frac{5}{16}$"
1	Back	$\frac{1}{2}$" x 4" x 22$\frac{5}{16}$"
2	Sides	$\frac{1}{2}$" x 4$\frac{1}{2}$" x 16"
2	Doors	$\frac{3}{4}$" x $\frac{3}{4}$" x 12$\frac{7}{16}$" x 18$\frac{3}{4}$"

Schedule of Materials • Worktop

No.	Item	Dimensions T W L
1	Top*	1$\frac{1}{8}$" x 25" x 96"
1	Top*	1$\frac{1}{8}$" x 23" x 96"
1	Beam	1$\frac{1}{2}$" x 3$\frac{1}{2}$" x 59"
1	Beam	1$\frac{1}{2}$" x 3$\frac{1}{2}$" x 56"

* Skin with $\frac{1}{4}$" hardboard

Schedule of Materials • Legs

No.	Item	Dimensions T W L
4	Verticles	1$\frac{1}{2}$" x 3$\frac{1}{2}$" x 27"
2	Top rails	1$\frac{1}{2}$" x 3$\frac{1}{2}$" x 16"
2	Stretchers	1$\frac{1}{2}$" x 3$\frac{1}{2}$" x 9"
2	Top plates	$\frac{3}{4}$" x 8" x 16"
4	Mounting brackets	$\frac{3}{4}$" x 4" x 16"
4	Mounting brackets	$\frac{3}{4}$" x 7" x 16"

Machinery and Equipment Selection

I knew I wanted to make general woodworking projects that would include furniture, cabinets, and smaller projects like jewelry boxes, toys, clocks, picture frames and bird feeders. I also knew that for materials, I'd be using both lumber (already planed to thickness) and various sheet goods like plywood or veneered medium-density fiberboard (MDF). Basically, I wanted to make boxes, big and small, which usually means making flat, straight, rectangular parts with square edges.

In my noble quest for the best prices and features, I made up an equipment list with "must buys" and "not necessary but nice" items. To give you an idea of how tough the shopping was, my five big-ticket items ate $434 of the $500 budget. These included a 10" benchtop table saw ($179), a good 2$\frac{1}{2}$-hp circular saw ($59), a 1$\frac{3}{4}$-hp plunge router ($90), a $\frac{3}{8}$" corded drill with keyless chuck ($59), and a random-orbit sander ($47). All these purchases were bought at everyday (not sale) prices and were brand-name products.

There were less expensive tools for sale, so you could probably meet or beat my choices. Features played a big part in my selections, and you need to think the same way. For example, I wanted a decent plunge router so I could cut precise mortises. Variable speed and reversing were important in selecting the drill, and the keyless chuck was a bonus. I really wanted a biscuit joiner, but then I remembered I could do much the same work with my router and a $\frac{5}{32}$" slot cutter.

The remaining hand tools, a few clamps and a couple measuring devices rounded out my purchases. Everything is listed in the adjoining table. Basic tools that everyone has (or should) aren't listed. Know anybody who doesn't have a hammer? Neither do I.

Shop in a Box

To get the most performance from my limited equipment and the most use from limited space, I designed a workstation that does all of the following:

- Provides huge extensions for the saw tabletop, providing greater capacity and safety;
- Features a built-in router table;
- Has ample storage for tools, equipment and supplies;
- Is a stable worktop for both machining and assembly;
- Can be set up in less than two minutes;
- Will accommodate dust collection for saw and router;

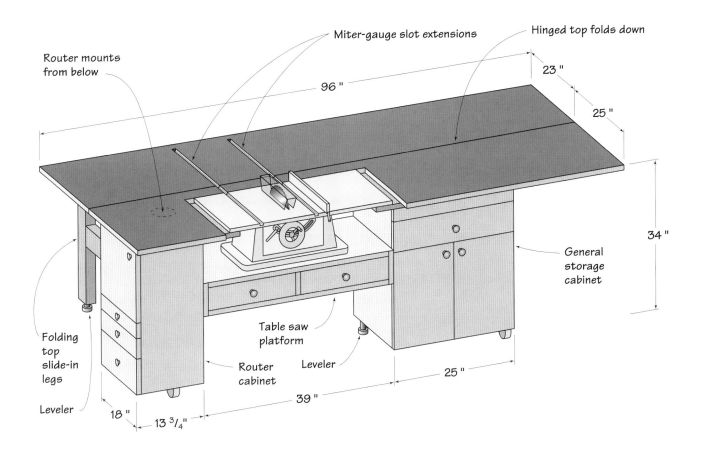

Router mounts from below

Miter-gauge slot extensions

Hinged top folds down

96 "

23 "

25 "

34 "

General storage cabinet

Folding top slide-in legs

Leveler

Table saw platform

Router cabinet

Leveler

25 "

18 "

13 3/4"

39 "

MACHINERY	Brand	Price
Table saw	Skil	$179.00
Circular saw	Skilsaw Classic 2.5 hp	$59.00
Drill	Ryobi DK38VSR	$59.00
Sander	Ryobi	$47.00
Plunge router	Ryobi 1.75 hp	$89.00
HAND TOOLS	**Brand**	**Price**
Tape measure	Lufkin 12'	$7.00
Combination square	Generic	$6.50
Pipe clamp ends	2 pair (at $8.50 ea.)	$17.00
Small steel bar clamps	2 units	$16.00
File (four in hand)	Nichols	$4.00
TOOLING	**Brand**	**Price**
Drill bits	Brad-point set	$12.00
Countersink		$3.00
Grand Total		**$498.50**

• Has multi-outlet plug strip for a convenient electric source;
• Has locking casters for easy rollout from storage;
• Folds in half to simplify storage.

For materials I used ¾" birch veneered MDF for the storage cabinets, ½" Baltic birch plywood for the drawer boxes, backs and fronts, 1⅛" particleboard for the top, and a few 2×4s as legs to support the folding portion of the top. I also used ¼" tempered hardboard for drawer bottoms and to skin the benchtop with a smooth, replaceable work surface. I used full-extension metal drawer slides and concealed hinges for the doors. Along with the casters, I spent nearly $250 to build the workstation, making it the most expensive "tool" in the project. However, I didn't include this cost in the $500 equipment and tool budget. If you choose lesser quality materials for the tops, cabinets and drawers, you could get the workstation's cost down to about $175.

Constructing the Mobile Shop

The principal components of my mobile shop are the folding top; a cabinet to the left of the saw, which is a combination router table and storage unit; a general storage cabinet to the right of the saw; and a shallow but stout two-drawer cabinet that is the table saw's platform. It also serves to bridge the two adjoining cabinets together. In the upright position, the hinged worktop is supported by a pair of slide-in-place legs.

I purchased my locking casters at the beginning so I was able to accurately establish the station's overall height of 34". This height matches most stationary equipment that may grace your shop in the future.

My first cutting task put my new circular saw and straightedge jig to work (see "First Build Three Jigs"), roughing out the cabinet parts from the 4×8 sheets of birch-veneered MDF (photo 1). For the most part, I was crosscutting the sheets, allowing about ½" extra length for later squaring and trim. You'll need a pair of sawhorses and some 2×4s

FIRST BUILD THREE JIGS

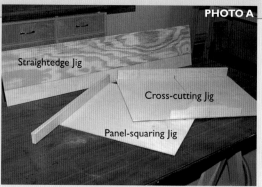

After assembling the benchtop saw, the first order of business is making three jigs. The first jig is used with a circular saw to provide a straight cut. It also helps for quick setups since the edge is essentially the line of the cut (photo A). This jig plays a major role in cutting the big sheets of MDF down to rough size so they can be cut safely and accurately on the table saw.

My straightedge jig, measuring 12" wide and 60" long, uses a piece of $\frac{1}{4}$" plywood on the bottom with a $\frac{3}{8}$" piece of plywood glued on top. When making this jig, be sure the bottom plywood edge nearest the blade and the top plywood edge that serves as the saw base's guide are absolutely parallel to each other. Don't use plywood pieces that are much thicker than recommended, because you begin to lose depth-of-cut capacity. Before gluing the plywood together, I cut a $\frac{1}{8}$" rabbet on the bottom side of the top piece's long edge. This gives chips and dust a place to go rather than interfering with the saw's straight cut.

My next two jigs are cutting sleds for the table saw. Both use the miter-gauge slot, and each will produce square cuts, a fundamental woodworking requirement. The panel-squaring jig (photo A) is used to make one square corner (the other corners can then be made square using the table saw fence).

To make this jig, I used another piece of $\frac{1}{4}$" plywood for the base, a precisely cut hardwood stick to exactly fit in the saw's miter-gauge slot, and another piece of hardwood for the fence. My sled bottom is $23\frac{1}{2}$" x 26" with a fence that's $2\frac{1}{2}$" x 32". As with the circular saw jig, I cut a small rabbet on the bottom edge of the fence for dust and chip clearance.

To assemble the jig, I set the hardwood stick in the left slot of the saw tabletop and put a bead of cyanoacrylate (Super Glue) down the center of the stick. With the blade raised as far as possible, set the jig's bottom carefully alongside the left side of the blade. The idea is to get the sled's bottom right edge in line with the blade. When positioning the bottom, let the stick on the bottom project out on both sides of the jig base. Clamp the stick and bottom in place and let the glue dry. After the adhesive is set, attach the fence. I did this very carefully, making sure the fence was exactly 90 degrees to the blade. I fastened it with screws, one near the blade edge and the second at the opposite edge. I made a slot for the second screw to allow for slight adjustments by pivoting the fence on the first screw until my angle was perfect. I then added more screws to secure it.

The second table saw sled (photo A) is very similar to the first and is used primarily for crosscutting pieces to length. Unlike the first jig, its fence is on the opposite side and backs up, rather than leads, the work. It also uses a stick in each miter-gauge slot. Because this sled's leading edge is sawed through, it's necessary to add a "bridge" between the bottom's sawed halves. This jig has a bottom that's $23\frac{1}{2}$"x 33". The fence is $2\frac{1}{2}$" x 32" and the bridge is 4" x 17".

I followed the same assembly procedure as before, first gluing the sticks in place (photo B), then attaching the fence, making sure it was 90 degrees to the blade (photo C). Since the bottom is glued to the sticks with the blade all the way down, I screwed the bridge in place after the glue dried. Next, I set the jig in the slots, turned on the saw and, while holding the jig down (watch where you put your hands!), raised the blade all the way up and into the jig. I turned the motor off and continued to hold the jig in place until the blade stopped coasting. After a couple test cuts using both new jigs, I was satisfied with their performance and was now ready to begin making the three cabinets for the workstation.

ATTACH THE SLED RUNNERS • To space the guides accurately, place them in the slots, apply glue, then set the sled in place.

SQUARE THE FENCE TO THE BLADE • I clamped boards in place to help align the sled perfectly.

to support the MDF.

I was pleased with the panel-squaring jig's performance (photo 2) and the little table saw's cutting ability. Granted, $\frac{3}{4}$" MDF isn't especially hard material, but not knowing what to expect from the saw, I found that a slow, steady feed rate produced acceptable results.

I was, however, unhappy with the shower of sawdust that covered me. This little saw spewed more dust than any table saw I'd ever operated. I remedied this annoyance by fabricating a zero-tolerance throat plate from $\frac{1}{4}$" plywood. This kept the dust out of my face and reminded me to put a ShopVac or dust collector on the top of my wish list.

With all the cabinet sides, backs and bottoms cut to rough size and one corner squared, I used the table saw fence to cut the remaining untrimmed edges (photo 3). This work went quickly, and I moved on to cutting rabbet joints. I always cut rabbets in the following way — first cutting with the panel run on edge (photo 4), followed by a second cut with the panel run flat (photo 5). Even if I had the money in my budget, I'd do this the same way and not buy a dado set.

The first cut is made with the table saw blade set $\frac{1}{4}$" from the fence. The blade height is slightly less than the thickness of material that the rabbet will receive (in this case, $\frac{3}{4}$"). The second cut is made with the fence set for the thickness of the material that the rabbet will receive, including the thickness of the saw blade. The blade height is set to fully cut away the waste piece to form the completed rabbet. The part being rabbeted is run flat on the saw. With the sides, bottom and top stretcher rabbeted, the back always fits neatly and plays a big role in squaring the cabinet. As I ran all my cabinet parts to form the rabbets, I again found the saw performing well. I was especially pleased to find that the saw's small fence was adequate and remained firmly in place.

I had also formed a rabbet as described above on the rail ends of the general storage cabinet. This required me to make a $\frac{1}{4}$" stopped dado on the inside front of the cabinet sides. I accomplished this with the regular saw

1 **BUILDING THE MOBILE WORKSTATION** • Begin the project by chopping the big sheets to manageable sizes with the straightedge jig.

2 **SQUARING CORNERS** • With the table saw panel-squaring jig, square one corner of each cabinet part, then mark it with a pencil.

blade, making two passes to achieve the $\frac{1}{4}$"-wide dado that was $\frac{3}{8}$" deep. I had made a reminder on my cutting list that making this dado would dedicate each side as either a right or left. The reminder meant that I had to set the fence for $9\frac{3}{4}$" and run the right side with the top edge against the fence in a normal method of pushing the work into the blade. However, to cut the left-side dado, I had to carefully lower the work over the blade, then push the work on through to complete the cut, again with the left side's top edge against the fence.

With all my cabinet joinery complete, I went directly to assembling my cases using glue and nails (photo 6). I like to clamp across the case when fastening to make sure the joint is pulled tight and my finished cabinet dimensions are achieved. Because I wanted the case that supports the table saw to be extra rigid, I glued and screwed it together.

To finish the MDF edges of the cabinet fronts, I used heat-sensitive iron-on birch veneer. (Of course, there's nothing budgeted for an iron, so borrow it from the laundry room.) To make sure you don't mess up the iron's bottom, use a piece of kraft paper under it. If you haven't used veneer tape before, you'll soon see that it's simple and efficient. The bottom is coated with hot-melt glue. With my iron set to high heat, the edging sticks down easily from a slow, but steady, pass over the length of veneer (photo 7). A flat file trims the tape overhang quickly and easily using the teeth on the edge of the file.

With my cabinets assembled, I proceeded to screw them all together. The plan calls for all three boxes to be flush in the back, so screw them together indexing off these surfaces (although technically the router cabinet back butts to the saw platform cabinet's left side). I measured down 9⅞" from the top of the cabinets to mark the location of the saw platform cabinet's top edge. After drilling eight clearance holes in the sides of the saw cabinet, I set the router cabinet on its face and carefully positioned the saw cabinet. I then screwed the two cabinets together (photo 8). Next, I positioned the general storage cabinet so that when I tipped the other attached cabinets over to be right side up, I could clamp the unattached case to the others (photo 9). I fine-tuned the location, reclamped it, then screwed the third cabinet to the first two.

Before attaching the casters, I took a length of 2×4 and screwed it to the back of the general storage cabinet and the side of the router cabinet so it was flush to the top edge of both. This very effectively completed the bridging of these

3 TRIM THE PANELS • Each panel is trimmed to final size using the saw fence and cutting opposite edges to the squared corner.

4 CUT RABBETS • The rabbets are cut by running the panel on edge against the fence, which is set to ¼" with the blade set about ¹¹⁄₁₆" high.

5 COMPLETE RABBETS After adjusting the fence and blade height, the rabbets are completed running the panel flat on the saw table. Be sure to stand to one side of the blade, since the piece being cut can shoot back when the cut is completed.

two cabinets and would also act as a "joist" for the worktop.

With my cabinet assembly finished, I bolted my locking swivel casters on the two end cabinet bottoms. Below the router cabinet, I positioned the casters in the center as close to the sides as possible. For the other cabinet, I attached them to the outside right corners.

Making the Top

Using my circular saw and straightedge jig, I split my heavy particleboard top lengthwise leaving one piece 25" wide. This piece covers the cabinets. Again using my straightedge jig and circular saw, I made a cutout in the top for the router base so it could attach directly to the ¼" tempered hardboard that will cover the particleboard subtop. I positioned the router cutout near the back left corner of the router cabinet to give maximum infeed space and ample room in front of the router. Next, I cut the tempered hardboard to the same width as the particleboard and, after aligning the edges, screwed it down to its subtop around the perimeter. I then made another cutout 20½"-wide by 37"-long for the table saw in this now sandwiched top. The cutout allowed for a 1" top overhang in the table saw, as well. The cut started 18" from the left (the router table end). I added more screws to the top at the perimeter of the cutout.

I drilled clearance holes through the cabinet stretchers, positioned the top over the cabinets leaving appropriate overhangs, and screwed it in place from inside the cabinets. The workstation was starting to look like something now.

I noticed that while the table saw top was flat enough, its molded plastic base wouldn't align with the larger surrounding worktop when fastened to its platform below. I overcame this problem by mounting wood brackets under the worktop overhang. This allowed me to shim the table saw top exactly where I wanted it — just a skosh above the surrounding worktop. Of course, I didn't want the saw suspended from the brackets, so I shimmed the saw base relative to the platform, then fastened the saw base in place.

6 **ASSEMBLE THE CABINETS** • Cabinets are assembled with glue and nails. A clamp pulls the parts together while fastening.

7 **VENEER THE FRONT EDGES** • After assembly, the front edges of the cabinet are finished with veneer that has hot-melt glue applied to the back side.

Next, I carefully extended the saw table's miter-gauge slots in the worktop hardboard by hand sawing, making my jigs even more useful. Before attaching the folding section of the top with a heavy-duty, continuous piano hinge, I fabricated the removable legs that would support it.

To make the legs, I cut my 2×4s to length (the exact length is dependent on the type of levelers you select) and glued up the assemblies using two no. 20 biscuits for each joint (photo 10). My router milled the biscuit slots using a 5⁄32" slot cutter in combination with a 7⁄8" bearing. This method of cutting biscuit

slots worked well and produced a strong joint.

To the top of both leg assemblies, I glued and screwed a ¾" MDF plate that's part of the sturdy, easy-on/easy-off leg system. The plate slides into a double-thickness MDF assembly that captures the leg plate on two sides (photo 11). I found that adding two pieces of typing paper under the capturing MDF assemblies added just the clearance needed for a snug, yet non-binding fit.

Before hinging the two tops together, I screwed the hardboard skin to the fold-down side of the particleboard subtop. Then I screwed the 6'-long continuous hinge to the top attached to the cabinets (photo 12). With the leg levelers installed and the legs in place, I set the folding top in position. Before fastening the hinge to the top, I adjusted the leg levelers until the seam of the two tops were flush along their length. Now I attached the other leaf of the hinge to the folding top.

The worktop was complete when I extended the miter slot grooves into the folding top. I did this using the straight-edge guide and the circular saw set to make a ¼"-deep cut through the hardboard.

Making the Doors and Drawers

With the project nearing completion, I sighted across it, table saw in place. The top looked as big and flat as an aircraft carrier. In fact, it's large enough to set up an auxiliary fence to the right of the blade and to crosscut to the center of an 8' sheet of plywood (photo 13).

It was a much easier task cutting out drawer parts and door fronts with the workstation fully assembled. Following my materials list, I cut my parts using the same procedures of rough-sizing, squaring one corner, then finish-cutting to size as I had done with the cabinet parts. I made rabbets on the drawer sides, using the two-cut system on my table saw. I also cut the grooves for the drawer bottom in the sides and sub-front, making two passes over the table saw blade.

I assembled the seven drawers with glue and nails, then slipped the bottoms in through the back, checked the drawers for square, then nailed the bottom into the drawer back. With one exception, all drawers were hung using full-extension, ball-bearing metal drawer slides. The drawer boxes, minus their screw-on finished fronts, were installed, two each in all three cabinets.

That seventh drawer box really isn't one at all, but a handy, removable dust bin below the router tabletop. I didn't want to use metal slides that would seize up from all the router dust, so I made this drawer just ¹⁄₁₆" smaller in width and length than the cabinet interi-

8 CABINET CONNECTION • The table saw platform cabinet is screwed to the back of the router cabinet.

9 ATTACH GENERAL STORAGE CABINET In turn, the general storage cabinet is screwed to the other two while held in place with a clamp.

10 LEG JOINTS • With no biscuit joiner in the budget, a router does the trick. Here, double biscuit leg joints are made using a ⁵⁄₃₂" slot cutter with a ⅞" bearing.

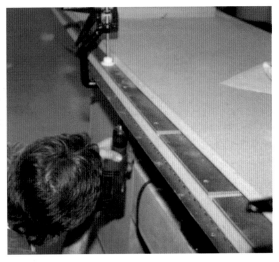

12 **INSTALL TOP HINGE** • The continuous hinge for the folding top was first attached to the fixed top.

11 **REMOVABLE LEGS** • The removable legs of the folding top slide into mating parts screwed to the top's underside.

13 **USE AN AUXILIARY FENCE** Width-of-cut capacity is enhanced with an auxiliary fence set parallel to the blade.

was complete. As I sanded the cabinets and then brushed on a clear finish, I started to plan my next projects. I'll need a shop-made router fence; some drawer inserts for more organized storage; some fixtures, perhaps for aids to clamping; and, of course, more jigs. I have lots of projects in mind and, as the budget allows, more tools and equipment to add. The Little Shop is going to get a lot of use.

Author's note: I found that after about a year, the unit had a tendency to sag between the two cabinets. This was due to the fact that much of the top is cut away where the saw is positioned. The saw platform cabinet is not deep enough to overcome the problem. The adjustable foot under the general storage cabinet works, but is less-than-convenient to use. You can overcome the problem by making the saw platform cabinet at least twice as deep, or add a 1/2"- or 3/4"-thick piece of plywood that runs behind the saw platform and screws securely to the general storage, router and saw platform cabinets.

or and screwed 1/4"-thick strips on the cabinet sides to work as drawer runners.

Next, I cut out the door and drawer fronts. The dimensions given for these parts are listed here and show finished sizes. When I use veneer tape, I deduct 1/32" for each veneer edge. My finished sizes allow for a 1/16" gap all around the doors and drawers.

To mount the fronts easily, I predrill clearance holes in the drawer subfronts and apply double-sided tape to the outside. I then carefully set the front in place, pull the drawer out, clamp it, then secure it with screws through the subfront. Any minor irregularities are

taken care of with the adjusting screw slots provided on the slides.

The doors were hung using concealed, European-type hinges. They offer adjustment in three directions, making them a dream to use once you understand how to mount and use them. Because mounting the hinges on the doors required a special and expensive drill bit, I took my doors to a local cabinet shop and had the six holes drilled.

After installing the door and drawer pulls, I mounted the fused electric outlet strip on the side of the router cabinet below the folding top. Except for sanding and finishing, the workstation

STORAGE TIPS

GREAT, FREE PARTS BINS
Once you're done changing the oil in your car or lawn mower, turn that empty plastic oil container upside down over some newspaper and let it drain completely. Use a utility knife to make small storage bins for nuts, bolts, screws and other items. You can either build a simple storage frame or purchase a tray to keep the bins neatly in place.

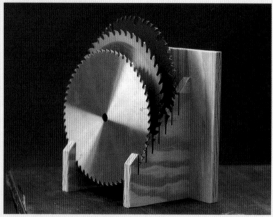

SAW BLADE STORAGE MADE E-Z • Sure, you could just drive a nail into your workshop wall and hang your saw blades on it like so many metal Frisbees. You could, but you shouldn't. If you're using good (which is to say "I'm in trouble if my wife ever finds out how much I'm paying for these . . . .") carbide-tipped blades, you need to remember that carbide is itself brittle. Bang a couple of blades together and you can chip those teeth easily. So build a rack along these lines from some $\frac{3}{4}$" plywood. Cut three pieces, then lay out the 45-degree angle on the two side pieces and cut them. Then cut slots about $1\frac{3}{4}$" to 2" deep, enlarging them a little bit if necessary so the blades slide easily into the rack. Leave enough material between the slots so the wood doesn't break away while cutting. Assemble with glue and screws and mount on a wall or place on your workbench.

GLUE'S CLUES • Speed up your parts and fastener finding. Use your hot-melt glue gun to stick a sample on the outside of the box, bag or storage compartment. This also means you'll always have at least one part of that size on hand no matter what, saving you some late-night hardware store runs.

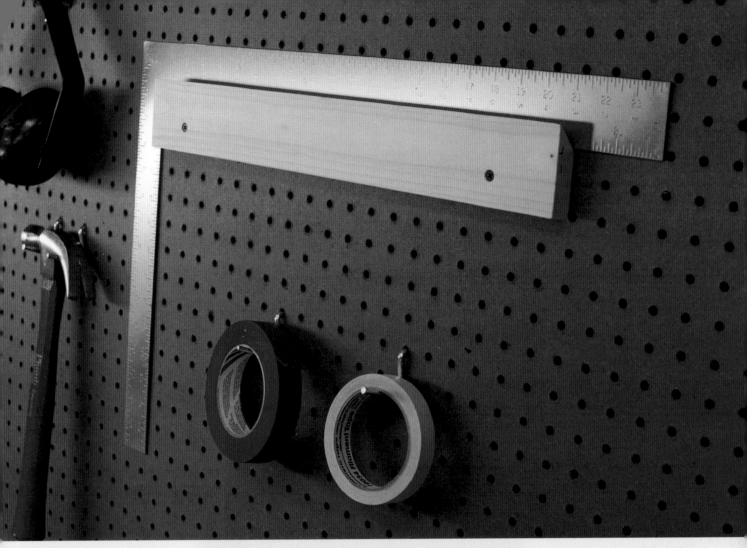

SQUARE HOLDER • Big framing squares are impossible to store neatly, it seems. We found a solution by mounting a piece of scrap to our shop wall. First, though, we cut a 45-degree angle on one edge to hold the square securely in place.

TOWEL RACK CLAMP HOLDER • Remodeling your bathroom and throwing away most of the old fittings and fixtures? Well, you might want to hold on to any old towel racks. Screwed to one end of your workbench or a wall, they provide a quick and convenient place to hang clamps. We use this one at the end of a workbench to get the clamps out of the way while we're preparing to glue up, yet have them quickly at hand when we're ready to go.

TO THE SHOWERS • Use pear-shaped metal shower curtain rings to hold nuts, washers, spare keys and other hard-to-organize hardware. The latching action keeps the pieces secure and easy to carry, yet unhooks quickly. They're just the right size to hang on a hook from your Peg-Board.

CRAYONS TO THE RESCUE • Save yourself some squinting and headscratching, and label the ends or face (or both) of lumber stored away. It saves a lot of shopping trips or digging through the stack when you'd rather be building.

CORD CARRIER • Extension cords are a workshop necessity. To keep them at hand and tangle-free, store them in a 5-gallon plastic bucket. Use a utility knife to cut a hole near the bottom, and thread the pronged plug through the hole from the inside. Now coil the rest of the extension cord into the bucket. Not only does this keep the cord under control, the bucket provides a handy carrier for the tools you'll be using.

LET'S GET VERTICAL
Short pieces of molding, dowel rods and pipe are annoyingly hard to store and keep organized. The solution is to fill a small cardboard box with cut-to-fit cardboard shipping tubes. You can get both at any office supply store, or you might find them in the trash at work. Sections of plastic plumbing pipe also work.

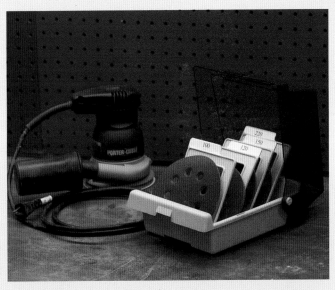

DISC STORAGE • Those old 5-¼" floppy computer disk storage boxes gathering dust in your closet make great organizers for sanding discs. The boxes come in a variety of sizes, some with dividers. A 6" disc fits perfectly and, if there are dividers, you can label them and be the complete neat freak.

PROTECT YOUR GLASS • It's easy to ruin a sheet of glass or mirror while it's being stored. So slip foam pipe insulation over the edges where it'll rest on the floor or on a shelf, and you'll have easy, cheap protection against chips and cracks. The foam also keeps the piece from slipping, giving you one less thing to worry about.

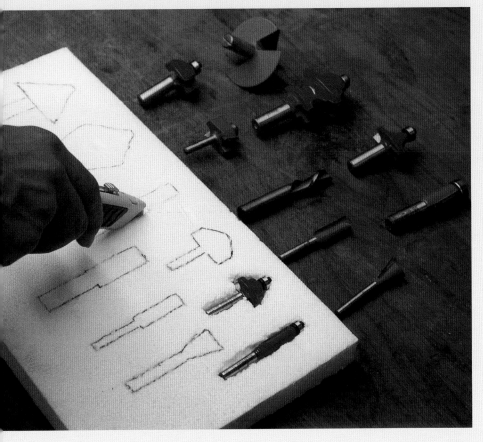

ROUTER BIT HOMES • Router bits are expensive, as you have probably learned; they shouldn't be allowed to bump into each other or anything else. So the next time you get a package at home or work, save the rigid packing foam. Use a utility knife to cut the foam to fit a drawer on your workbench. Then cut out separate compartments for all your router bits — and the ones you expect to get someday soon. You can also use stiff grades of foam rubber to get the same results.

Little Shop
Mark II

F our years ago, we published plans for The Little Shop That Could, an economical, small yet functional, portable workstation. Stocked with basic tools that cost less than $500, the concept was to get you in the woodworking door. *Popular Woodworking* editor Steve Shanesy, father of the Little Shop, made some hard fiscal decisions about what equipment to buy, not always choosing what he preferred, but what was within budget. Since that time, the Little Shop has produced 10 projects for the magazine, using only those tools. We decided it was time to upgrade. The result is the Little Shop Mark II. It's still designed for tight quarters, but we've spent a bit more on tools to allow more versatility and precision.

I tried to carry on the tradition of being as frugal as possible, without sacrificing quality. A budget of $1,000 was decided on as an acceptable amount to purchase everything needed, while keeping me from whining about not having "vital" tools. We also wanted to use parts and tools from the original Little Shop as a starting point.

I decided to use the two larger cabinets from the original Little Shop and simply add a new cabinet to support the new saw and some other power tool goodies. If you built the original Little Shop and want to build the Mark II version, simply substitute the new middle cabinet for the old one. For those of you who are visiting the Little Shop for the first time, there are drawings and sched-

The original Little Shop from the July 1996 issue. The project was so popular, the magazine sold out of copies of that issue.

ules for all the cabinets. This center cabinet makeover took place because of an unforeseen design flaw. The height of the original center cabinet couldn't adequately support the entire Little Shop and it began to splay. I designed the new cabinet to hold more weight, to store more stuff and to roll around on some heavier-duty casters.

The first and most critical tool addressed was the table saw. While the original Skil benchtop saw was a star player, I wanted the advantages of a contractor saw: namely more power, a longer arbor for dado heads and molding cutters, a better fence and more cutting capacity. Before you start calling me a whiner like Steve did, consider this: I

compare woodworking to my hobby, playing guitar. For years, I struggled on cut-rate, lousy instruments. My family will attest to the struggling part. That was until the day I dropped some serious coin on a Fender Telecaster. The doors of music making were suddenly thrown wide, and I knew that I'd be making hits in no time. Seriously, on a better instrument, I began to practice more. My skills improved, and I acquired the ability to play without offending people.

I searched high and low for a saw that would provide the right combination of price and capabilities. The Grizzly G1022 contractor saw ($375 + $60 shipping) fit the bill. I added the optional 70" fence extension tubes ($60) for wider cuts and to make room on the cabinet for a router table fence. The Ryobi plunge router from the first Little Shop also performed well, but it had a ¼" collet. The natural upgrade was the Porter-Cable 693PK fixed/ plunge router base kit ($179), which has both ¼" and ½" collets, and the fixed base will mount nicely in the router table section of the Mark II. Tired of cutting biscuits with my router, I decided to purchase the Freud JS102 ($117). The outfeed table on the original was a good idea, but Steve hadn't used a Black & Decker Workmate ($98 each) before then. The obvious utility provided by these ingenious sawhorse, clamp, tool-stand contraptions was hard to ignore. I added some torsion boxes to bring the height to that of the finished height on the Mark II, so I have two sturdy, folding outfeed tables. This gives a grand total of $987 before taxes. Not bad.

Construction

The case construction is the same rabbeted-sides style as the original Little Shop except that instead of nailing the case together, I used screws and glue for added strength. The new table saw works fine sitting on one of the Workmates until the case is made.

Begin construction by cutting out all of the parts for the tops. I substituted these tops for the cast-iron open wings on the saw because dust would inevitably settle through the holes in the

wings. And cleaning it would be difficult in the confined spaces under the saw. Start the tops by nailing the buildup to the underside of the tops. Make sure to keep it flush and square. Cut plastic laminate (check your yellow pages for local cabinetmaker supply stores) 1" bigger than the tops in both dimensions. Attach the laminate with contact cement and rout flush. Using a sanding block, sand the edges to smooth out any irregularities, and begin cutting ¾"×1½" stock to edge the tops. Use biscuits to align the edging, then glue and clamp in place. Try to keep the edging as flush to the top as possible. When the glue dries, clean up any edging that sticks above the top with a block plane and sand the edges. Apply three coats of Danish oil as a finish.

Attach the Tops

When unpacking the saw, one nice thing you'll realize is that the only assembly necessary is attaching the motor and fence bars. Grizzly sends a base with the saw, but it's not necessary for Mark II construction. You can't buy the unit without the base so consider it a bonus stand for some future machine in your shop.

To attach the tops, first install threaded inserts into the edge of the top. See the photo for details on this procedure. Use a board, on edge, of appropriate height to prop up the end of the top while bolting the top flush to the saw table. Repeat the same procedure

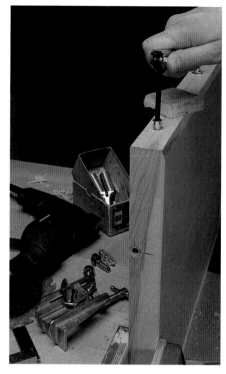

Measure the center locations of the existing holes on the saw table and the fence bars. There are five threaded insert locations per top. Next, drill the ⅜" receiving holes for the inserts. It helps to use a doweling jig, but it's not necessary. Make sure you measure every hole on both sides. They aren't located in exactly the same place.

for the small top.

The extra-long fence bars require some modifications to keep the Mark II's large, right-side top sturdy. Drill two ¼" holes in each bar at 6" and 22" from the far end. Enlarge the outside holes in the

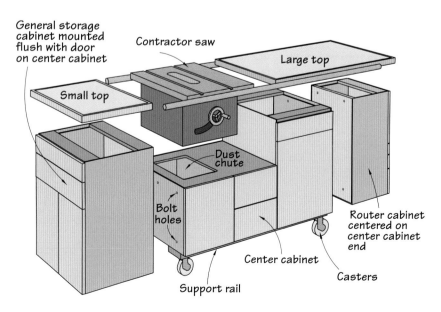

General storage cabinet mounted flush with door on center cabinet

Contractor saw

Large top

Small top

Dust chute

Bolt holes

Center cabinet

Router cabinet centered on center cabinet end

Casters

Support rail

Use spacers to set the height of each slide accurately. Start with the highest drawer and work your way down. The easiest way to do this is to attach the drawer slide to the drawer. Lay out in the cabinet exactly where you want the drawers to go. Then place the cabinet part of the slide on the drawer. Measure where the bottom of the slide is in relation to the bottom edge of the drawer. Subtract this from the drawer height inside the cabinet and that's the spacer height.

Schedule of Materials • New Center Cabinet

No.	Item	Dimensions T W L	Material
1	Large top	3/4" x 25 1/2" x 41 1/2"	Plywood
1	Small top	3/4" x 25 1/2" x 17 1/2"	Plywood
3	Buildup strips	3/4" x 4" x 96"	Plywood
4	Solid edging strips	3/4" x 1 1/2" x 96"	Maple
CENTER CASE			
1	Small end	3/4" x 23 3/4" x 16"	Plywood
1	Large end	3/4" x 23 3/4" x 27 1/2"	Plywood
1	Small partition	3/4" x 23 1/4" x 14 1/2"	Plywood
1	Large partition	3/4" x 23 1/4" x 26 3/4"	Plywood
1	Vertical divider	3/4" x 23 1/4" x 21 1/4"	Plywood
1	Dust shelf	1/4" x 23" x 14"	Plywood
1	Top	3/4" x 23 3/4" x 28 1/2"	Plywood
1	Bottom	3/4" x 23 3/4" x 47"	Plywood
1	Case back	1/2" x 27" x 47"	Plywood
2	Case rails	3/4" x 4" x 18 1/2"	Plywood
1	Drawer rail	3/4" x 4" x 18"	Plywood
2	Support rails	1 1/2" x 5 1/2" x 47 1/2"	Pine
1	Large door	3/4" x 19" x 22 1/2"	Plywood
1	Small door	3/4" x 14 1/2" x 15 7/8"	Plywood
ROLLOUTS			
4	Backs	1/2" x 2" x 12"	Plywood
4	Fronts	1/2" x 2" x 12"	Maple
4	Bottoms	1/4" x 12" x 22 1/4"	Plywood
8	Sides	1/2" x 2" x 22 3/4"	Plywood
LOWER DRAWERS			
2	False fronts	3/4" x 8" x 13 3/4"	Plywood
4	Fronts & backs	1/2" x 6" x 12"	Plywood
4	Sides	1/2" x 6" x 22 1/2"	Plywood
2	Bottoms	1/4" x 12" x 22"	Plywood
UPPER DRAWER			
1	False front	3/4" x 4 1/4" x 19"	Plywood
2	Front & back	1/2" x 2 3/4" x 16"	Plywood
2	Sides	1/2" x 2 3/4" x 22 3/4"	Plywood
1	Bottom	1/4" x 16" x 22 1/4"	Plywood

bars to 1/2" to clear a screw bit holder. Use no. 10×1 1/2" wood screws and spacers between the bar and the top to secure the large top at these four holes. Adjust the wooden spacers until the fence works smoothly.

Case Construction

Once the tops are flush, cut out the case parts according to the schedule of materials. Cut 1/2"×3/4" rabbets in the top and bottom edges of the case ends and the top of the large partition. Use the two-step table saw method for these rabbets, standing the part on its edge for the first cut, then laying it flat and cutting the rest of the rabbet. These rabbets accept the rails, top and bottom pieces. The last rabbet cut is the 1/2"×1/2" rabbet for the back.

To rout the 1/4"-deep dadoes in the case, set up a pattern-routing bit with the bearing on top, using one of the partitions as a straightedge. It's now a simple matter of using screws and glue to assemble the case. Use this sequence for the most trouble-free assembly: Assemble the large partition and the top, followed by the small end and small partition, the bottom, the large end and the rails. Keep the inside of the back rabbet flush during assembly. It's easier to flush up the front edges that way. Make sure

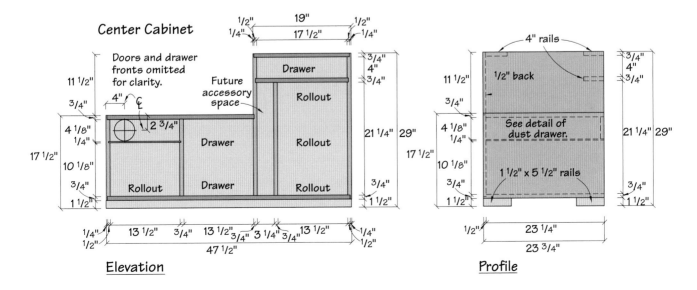

Elevation

Profile

TORSION BOXES

One decision I made early in the Little Shop re-design: eliminate the full-length outfeed table. It was a bit awkward to set up, and I'd rather have a work table at a lower height.

Using the Workmates, clutter is kept off the saw, and the clamping vises can be used during furniture assembly. With the addition of torsion boxes, they make adequate, lightweight, outfeed tables at the same level as the table saw top.

The boxes are made by nailing together a plywood frame like a stud frame in house construction. Offset stretchers are nailed in place between the studs, then plywood skins are nailed to the outsides.

Cut out the parts listed in the schedule. Nail the frame together: stand the four short frame parts on end and nail the long frame part onto them. Use the stretchers as spacers for nailing. Next, nail the $\frac{1}{4}$" plywood skin on one side. Clamp the two clamping rails into a Workmate using the Workmate's third spacer. Place the partially assembled box on the Workmate and flush the rails on one end. Leave $\frac{1}{2}$" overhang on the side with the handles. Mark the locations of the rails on the $\frac{1}{4}$" plywood and turn the box over. Drill pilot holes into the plywood, lining the box up on the pencil marks, and attach the rails. Attach the other skin on the top side of the box. Finish-sand and apply two coats of finish.

Depending on the fit you want, you might take a $\frac{1}{16}$" cut off of the Workmate's middle spacer width. As designed, the riser boxes are $\frac{1}{4}$" lower than the saw table's height, so you can adjust for irregularities in the floor and still have a su face level to the saw table.

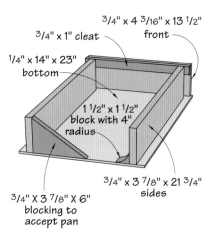

Use this diagram to lay out the support blocking for sheet metal in the dust diverter. When you've built the drawer, take an oversize piece of sheet metal and start by attaching it to the cleat on the back of the drawer front. Gently force the metal into the mold and screw in place. Tap the edge over with a hammer and screw this lip into place. Attach door weather stripping to the parts of the diverter that may leak dust when it's slid in or out of the case.

Schedule of Materials
Torsion Boxes

No.	Item	Dimensions T W L
2	Sides	$\frac{3}{4}$" x $3\frac{1}{2}$" x 30"
3	Stretchers	$\frac{3}{4}$" x $3\frac{1}{2}$" x 9"
4	Studs	$\frac{3}{4}$" x $3\frac{1}{2}$" x $22\frac{1}{2}$"
2	Skins	$\frac{1}{4}$" x 24" x 30"
2	Clamping rails	$\frac{1}{2}$" x $1\frac{3}{4}$" x 30"

to keep the case square as you go. Screw the back in last.

If you need to make the two outer cases, do so now using the schedule at right. Construction is the same as outlined for the new section, using $\frac{1}{2}$"x$\frac{3}{4}$" rabbets in the ends, otherwise continue on.

The next step is to apply iron-on edge banding to the front edges of the case. Finish the case by attaching the casters to the bottom support rails.

The Dust Diverter

Dust collection can be accommodated by building a small diverter out of sheet metal and plywood. It's removable for cleaning when (not if) you drop the arbor nut into the saw. See the photo and drawing above for details.

Drawers and Doors

After leveling the case on a flat surface, make the drawers. (You'll notice that the drawer openings for the new section are all $13\frac{1}{2}$" wide, with one exception. This makes cutting out drawers and roll-out shelves much easier.) Use a $\frac{1}{4}$"x$\frac{1}{2}$" rabbet cut on the drawer sides, and use a $\frac{1}{4}$"x$\frac{1}{4}$" groove, $\frac{1}{2}$" up from the bottom edge for the bottoms. Install the drawers with standard $\frac{1}{2}$"x22" drawer slides.

Next, edgeband the doors and drawer fronts, then hang the doors using European hinges. These are full overlay hinges, which means that the front of the door completely overhangs the edge of the cabinet. European hardware is designed to use a hole created by a 32mm Forstner bit. A $1\frac{3}{8}$" Forstner bit is close enough. The plate gets mounted to the inside of the cabinet per the manufacturer's instructions. Attach the drawer fronts with screws through the

Use a European hinge that will allow the door to swing free of the rollout shelves and not hit the adjoining cabinets.

Supplies

Available from Lee Valley Tools, (800) 871-8158, www.leevalley.com:
4- Casters, item #00K2001, $10.95 each
10- Threaded Inserts, item #00N1025, $1.30

Available from Rockler, (800) 279-4441, www.rockler.com:
2 pr.- Hinges, item #34595, $13.95 a pair
7 pr.- Drawer Slides, item #34876, $5.99 a pair

Available from Grizzly, (800) 523-4777, www.grizzlyindustrial.com:
1- G1022 Table Saw with 70" extension tubes (G1187), $494.95

Schedule of Materials
Little Shop Mark II

No.	Item	Dimensions T W L
ROUTER CABINET		
2	Ends	$3/4$" x 13" x 29"
1	Back	$3/4$" x 17" x $28^3/4$"
1	Bottom	$3/4$" x 13" x 17"
1	Top stretcher (front)	$3/4$" x 4" x 17"
1	Door	$3/4$" x $17^1/2$" x $14^5/8$"
1	Drawer front	$3/4$" x $17^1/2$" x 3"
1	Drawer subfront	$1/2$" x $2^1/2$" x $15^7/16$"
1	Drawer back	$1/2$" x 2" x $15^7/16$"
2	Drawer sides	$1/2$" x $2^1/2$" x 12"
1	Drawer bottom	$1/4$" x $11^3/4$" x $15^7/16$"
1	Drawer front	$3/4$" x $17^1/2$" x $3^7/8$"
1	Drawer subfront	$1/2$" x $3^1/2$" x $14^1/2$"
1	Drawer back	$1/2$"x 3" x $14^1/2$"
2	Drawer sides	$1/2$" x $3^1/2$" x 12"
1	Drawer bottom	$1/4$" x $11^3/4$" x $14^1/2$"
1	Drawer front	$3/4$" x $17^1/2$" x 7"
1	Drawer subfront	$1/2$" x 6" x $14^1/2$"
1	Drawer back	$1/2$" x $5^1/2$" x $14^1/2$"
1	Drawer side	$1/2$" x 6" x 12"
1	Drawer bottom	$1/4$" x $11^3/4$" x $14^1/2$"
GENERAL STORAGE CABINET		
2	Ends	$3/4$" x $17^1/4$" x 29"
1	Back	$3/4$" x $24^1/2$" x $28^1/2$"
1	Bottom	$3/4$" x $17^1/4$" x $24^1/2$"
2	Stretchers	$3/4$" x 4" x $24^1/2$"
1	Rail	$3/4$" x 4" x $24^1/4$"
1	Drawer front	$3/4$" x 25" x 4"
1	Drawer subfront	$1/2$" x 3" x 22"
1	Drawer back	$1/2$" x $2^1/2$" x 22"
2	Drawer sides	$1/2$" x 3" x 16"
2	Drawer bottoms	$1/4$" x $15^3/4$" x 22"
1	Drawer front	$3/4$" x 25" x $5^3/4$"
1	Drawer subfront	$1/2$" x $4^1/2$" x 22"
1	Back	$1/2$" x 4" x 22"
2	Sides	$1/2$" x $4^1/2$" x 16"
2	Doors	$3/4$" x $12^7/16$" x $18^3/4$"

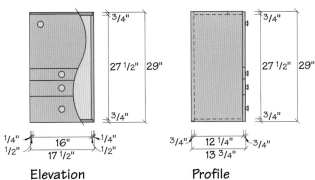

Router cabinet

Elevation — 27 1/2" 29" — 3/4", 3/4" — 1/4" 16" 1/4" 1/2" 17 1/2" 1/2"

Profile — 27 1/2" 29" — 3/4", 3/4" — 3/4" 12 1/4" 3/4" 13 3/4"

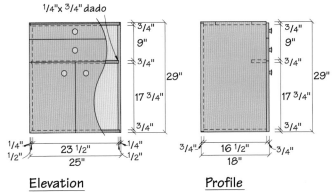

General storage cabinet

1/4"x 3/4" dado

Elevation — 3/4" 9" 3/4" 29" 17 3/4" 3/4" — 1/4" 23 1/2" 1/4" 1/2" 25" 1/2"

Profile — 3/4" 9" 3/4" 29" 17 3/4" 3/4" — 3/4" 16 1/2" 3/4" 18"

drawer boxes. Attach the drawer/door pulls and set the case on the floor.

Once you get everything fit, it's time for finishing the cabinet and innards with two coats of clear lacquer. Take all of the hardware off to do this as it might gum up the slides and hinges, and it leaves unfinished spots on the drawers and doors.

Making the Whole from the Parts

It's now time to attach the two outer cases to the center case. Attach the large case to the left end of the center case with the drawer/doors facing to the left. Attach the small case centered on the right end doors facing to the right. This will house the router table assembly. Once you attach the top to the cases, the whole unit is quite sturdy.

Our redesign of this historic tool chest brings it up-to-date for today's power tools.

Benjamin Seaton's **Tool Chest**

This eighteenth-century English tool chest is one of the more interesting mysteries in the history of woodworking. Unlike other tool chests of its day, this chest and its tools — which are now in the Guildhall Museum in Rochester, England — went virtually unused and are in the same condition as when they were new in 1796.

How did this chest survive? Why didn't Benjamin Seaton, the maker of the chest, ever use his tools? Was he planning to come to the New World to begin a cabinetmaking business? While historical records cannot fully answer these questions, they do tell an interesting tale of a would-be woodworker.

Benjamin was born in 1775, the son of a cabinetmaker and church elder. When Benjamin turned 21, his father bought him a complete and very expensive set of woodworking tools, and on January 1, 1797, Benjamin began building this chest to house them. He finished it April 15. Three months later, Benjamin made an inventory of the chest's contents, which survives to this day. The Guildhall Museum suggests that Benjamin was preparing to emigrate to America. However, Benjamin remained in Chatham and tended to the family business after his father's death in 1811.

Benjamin died in 1830, and his will describes him as a cabinetmaker, upholsterer, auctioneer and undertaker. His chest remained in his family, with the tools intact, until it was given to the museum in 1910.

A few years ago, the Tool and Trades History Society in England published a book, *The Tool Chest of Benjamin Seaton* (now out of print). After reading the book, I became convinced that this tool chest would be great for a set of twentieth-century tools — with a few modifications. So I built one. And it didn't take three and a half months.

The large outer case holds many of my modern handheld power tools: a jigsaw, drill, router, circular saw, random-orbit sander, belt sander and biscuit joiner (with room to spare). The removable case (called a till), with its lids and drawers, holds just about every hand tool a well-equipped shop needs. If I wanted to go overseas and set up a cabinet shop, I could load the chest on a steamer and go. Instead, the large case now sits on the floor next to my bench, protecting my power tools until I need them. The till sits on top of my bench, keeping my hand tools within arm's reach. It's a perfect system for a small shop that's low on both space and built-in cabinets.

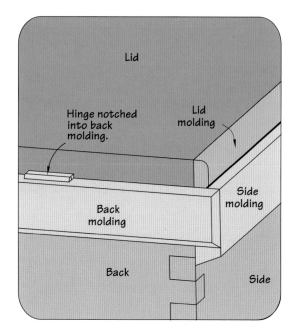

Lid

Hinge notched into back molding.

Lid molding

Side molding

Back molding

Back

Side

Detail of back corner of case

Schedule of Materials • Tool Chest

No.	Item	Dimensions T W L	Material
2	Sides	$7/8"$ × $23\,1/4"$ × $23\,1/2"$	Pine
2	Front & back	$7/8"$ × $23\,1/4"$ × $35\,1/2"$	Pine
1	Top	$7/8"$ × $23\,1/2"$ × $35\,1/2"$	Pine
1	Bottom	$7/8"$ × $22\,5/8"$ × $34\,5/8"$	Pine
2	Cleats	$1\,1/2"$ × $4\,3/4"$ × $14\,3/4"$	Pine
2	Runners	$1\,1/4"$ × $3\,1/16"$ × $21\,3/4"$	Pine
	Bottom molding	11' of $3/4"$ × $2\,5/8"$	molding
	Top molding	11' of $7/8"$ × $2\,1/2"$	molding
	Lid molding	11' of $1/2"$ × $1\,3/8"$	molding

Seaton's Tool Till

No.	Item	Dimensions T W L	Material
2	Sides	$3/4"$ × $11"$ × $11"$	Veneered pine
1	Back	$3/4"$ × $11"$ × $32\,3/4"$	Veneered pine
1	Top	$3/4"$ × $11"$ × $33\,1/2"$	Walnut
1	Bottom	$3/4"$ × $10\,5/8"$ × $32\,3/4"$	Pine
1	Front	$3/4"$ × $2\,1/2"$ × $32"$	Veneered pine
3	Horiz. dividers	$3/8"$ × $10\,5/8"$ × $32\,3/4"$	Pine
2	Vert. dividers, top	$3/8"$ × $2\,1/8"$ × $5"$	Pine
2	Vert. dividers, mid.	$3/8"$ × $2\,3/8"$ × $5"$	Pine
2	Vert. dividers, bot.	$3/8"$ × $3\,5/8"$ × $5"$	Pine

Supplies

Available from Lee Valley Tools,
800-871-8158, www.leevalley.com:

1 Chest Lock - $10.95	Item #12K04.01
Case hinges - $20.25 pr.	Item #00D03.04
Till Hinges - $17.50 pr.	Item #00D06.02
Flush Ring Pull - $12.50	Item #00L02.02

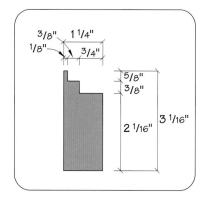

Detail of till runner

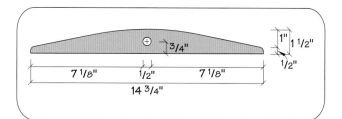

Detail of cleat

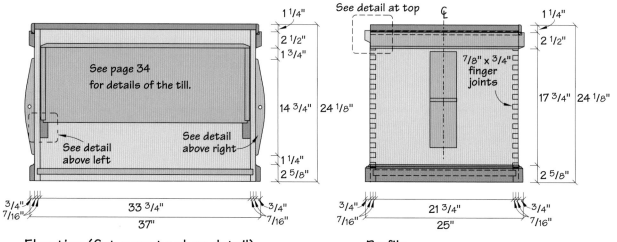

See page 34 for details of the till.

See detail above left

See detail above right

1 1/4"
2 1/2"
1 3/4"
14 3/4"
24 1/8"
1 1/4"
2 5/8"

3/4"
7/16"
33 3/4"
3/4"
7/16"
37"

Elevation (Cut away to show detail)

See detail at top

$7/8"$ × $3/4"$ finger joints

1 1/4"
2 1/2"
17 3/4"
24 1/8"
2 5/8"

3/4"
7/16"
21 3/4"
3/4"
7/16"
25"

Profile

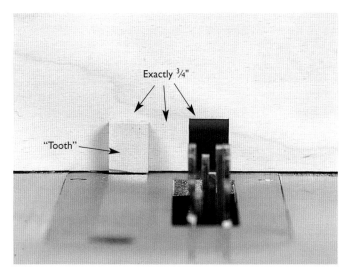

Exactly ¾"

"Tooth"

Once you make the first cut on the edge of a board, put that notch over the tooth.

1 FINGER-JOINT JIG • The trick to finger joints is to make sure the width of your dado stack is precisely the same as the space between the dado stack and the stop, which I'll call the "tooth." The tooth should also be exactly as wide as your dado stack. Begin by screwing a large piece of plywood (8" high, about 25" long) to your table saw's miter gauge. Set up your dado stack to the desired dimension and run your jig through the saw. Take the jig off the saw and attach the tooth to the jig with glue and screws. A good bond is essential.

2 CUT THE JOINTS • It might seem a little scary to hold 39"-long boards on edge on your table saw. Feel free to clamp your work to the fence you screwed to your miter gauge, though this will slow you down a bit. If you proceed slowly and carefully — and your table saw's table is sufficiently waxed — you shouldn't have a problem. Once you cut the first space, pick up the board and place that space over the tooth in your jig. Then run the work through the saw again.

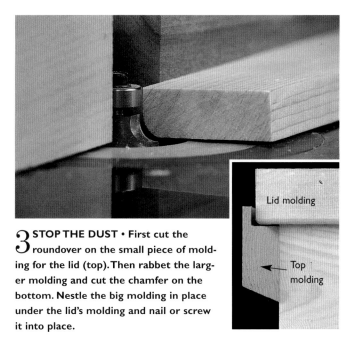

Lid molding

Top molding

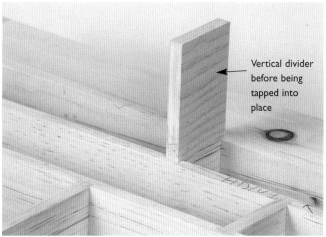

Vertical divider before being tapped into place

3 STOP THE DUST • First cut the roundover on the small piece of molding for the lid (top). Then rabbet the larger molding and cut the chamfer on the bottom. Nestle the big molding in place under the lid's molding and nail or screw it into place.

4 VERTICAL DIVIDERS • Add these after your till is assembled. Try to make the grain run up and down on these pieces to minimize the chances your case will break open when the wood begins to move. A little glue on the front ends of these dividers is all you need.

Finger Joints

Constructing the outer case is pretty simple. Finger joints join the four sides; the bottom is captured by a groove in all four sides. The molding is nailed or screwed to the exterior. The lid has a small piece of molding attached to it that acts as a dust seal.

Begin building the case by gluing up the ⅞"-thick panels for the sides, top and bottom. (Benjamin was lucky enough to have some 24"-wide pine boards and didn't have to glue up his sides.) Now make the jig to cut your ¾" ×⅞"-deep finger joints. Take your time with the jig because a little precision and patience will result in joints that won't split or beg for putty.

Cut Your Joints

Now that the jig is built, it's time to cut the joints. The trick with finger joints is to get all of the "fingers" and "spaces" to line up and mate correctly. If one board begins with a finger, then its mate must begin with a space. To make a board that begins with a finger, place it on end on your table saw against the tooth on the jig and make your cut. To begin a board with a space, place a spacer between the dado stack and tooth. I used some scrap finger joints that I ran as a test with this jig; these worked great. Place your board on end against this spacer; run it through the saw. Remove the spacer and cut the remainder of the joints on that edge.

Now cut the $7/16$"-deep by $7/8$"-wide grooves in the sides that hold the bottom in place. The grooves should be 1" up from the bottom edge. You can stop these grooves before you cut into your finger joints, and finish the grooves with a chisel. Or you can just run these grooves right through your joints — after all, they will be covered by the molding on the outside of the case.

Assemble the case using glue on the finger joints. Allow the bottom to float in its groove. Clean off as much glue squeeze-out as you can. Clamp and allow your case to dry.

Begin making the molding by routing a small ogee profile on the bottom molding pieces. Miter the pieces, then attach them with nails or screws. (Benjamin used screws that he recessed into the wood and then covered with putty.)

Dust Seal

Dust and grime have never been good for tools, and eighteenth-century cabinetmakers went to extreme lengths to keep their tools separated from dirt. Benjamin used a simple but effective seal (photo 3, previous page). Begin making the seal by cutting the lid to size and mortising the hinges into the case and lid.

Now rout a $1/4$" roundover on the three pieces of molding for the lid. Miter and nail this molding to the front and sides of the lid.

The second piece of molding adds another layer of protection. Begin by cutting a $9/16$"×$1/2$" rabbet into one edge of the molding. You also could use a roundnose bit in a router to cut a profile that will nest with the roundover on the lid's molding. Next cut a 25-degree bevel on the bottom of the four pieces of molding. Miter three pieces of mold-

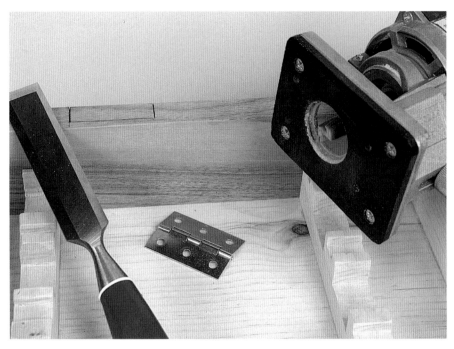

5 MORTISE YOUR HINGES • Using a straight bit in a router or trimmer is a great way to cut the mortises for your hinges. You just have to be careful not to go over the edge you marked, which is an easy mistake to make. The easiest way to prevent this problem is to pare the edges with a chisel or a knife. When your bit gets near the pared edge, it shears away, leaving a square edge.

ing and nail or screw them to the front and sides of the case. Do not miter the back edges of the molding that goes on the sides. Cut these flush with the case. Now make the molding for the back. This molding is different because it helps seal the back of the case and acts as a stop for the lid. It's pretty ingenious. Take a piece of molding back to the table saw and rip off the rabbet. Now attach this molding to the back, flush to the top edge of the case. You'll have to cut notches in the molding for the barrels of the three hinges that hold the lid. Screw and glue this molding to the back.

Now cut the cleats for the sides that hold the rope handles. Use a band saw to cut them to rough shape and sand them down. Then drill a $1/2$" hole through the center for the rope. Attach the cleats with screws.

If you want to add a lock to your chest, now is the best time. I used a small full-mortise chest lock. You can now add the dividers for your power tools at the bottom of the case. Fill all your screw holes with water putty and finish-sand the exterior of the case to

120 grit. Paint the exterior blue. Now it's time to turn your attention to the till.

Build the Till

The till is a box that's divided into four "stories" by wide $3/8$"-thick pine boards dadoed into the back and sides. You access the top level by opening the lid of the box. The bottom three levels are for nine drawers. I wanted my till to weigh very little, so I made the case from pine veneered with walnut (have lots of clamps ready). The top is solid walnut; the bottom is plain pine.

Begin building the till by cutting the boards to size and then cutting $3/8$"×$3/4$" rabbets in the sides for the back. Now cut $3/8$"×$3/8$" rabbets in the sides and back to capture the $3/4$" bottom. The bottom sticks out of the case $3/8$", which allows the till to slide on runners in the large case.

Now cut the $3/8$"×$3/8$" grooves in the sides for the three horizontal dividers in locations (see diagram). Then cut the $3/16$"×$3/16$" grooves for the six vertical dividers that separate the drawers.

Dry-assemble the case. When everything fits, assemble the till with nails

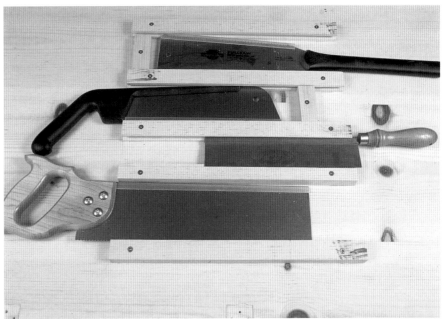

6 **RUNNERS** • When your runners are finished they should look like three steps. The top step is $^1/_8$" thick and $^5/_8$" high. The second step is $^3/_8$" thick and $^3/_8$" high. The third step is the remainder of the board. See the diagram for all the dimensions for the runners.

7 **SAW HOLDER** • Make sure when you set up your strips that you position your saws with the teeth facing up. This prevents them from getting damaged when you open the lid.

and glue. Attach the vertical dividers last. Use only nails when attaching the horizontal dividers to allow for wood movement. Attach the vertical dividers with a little glue and a dead-blow mallet (photo 4).

Now, using nails and glue, attach the front piece at the top that encloses the top tool area. Cut your top to finished size and cut a detail on the top edge to soften the look. I routed a $^3/_{16}$"-deep by 1" chamfer on all four edges. A table saw also would do this job nicely. Finally, I mortised a flush ring-pull into the lid to make opening the lid easier.

Till Details

Swage your hinges and then mortise them into the till and the lid (photo 5). Start dividing up the top tool area for the hand tools that you reach for most often. I made a rack for my chisels and cubbyholes for my small planes. Finally, I built two holders that flip up. One holds my drill bits, the other holds my screwdrivers and a marking gauge.

If you've veneered your case, now is the time to add a piece of veneer to the

front piece and to cover all the other pine edges that show. I used walnut veneer tape for all the dividers. This tape costs about $3 for an 8' length. After you've veneered the entire till, fill your nail holes with putty and sand the case.

Now cut your drawers. Mark all your pieces because you'll have 40 pieces to keep track of. The nine drawers are all assembled in the same manner. On the $^3/_4$"-thick drawer fronts, cut a $^3/_8$"×$^3/_8$" rabbet on each end. On the $^3/_8$"-thick sides, cut a $^3/_{16}$"-deep by $^3/_8$" wide dado for the back. Then cut a $^3/_{16}$"-deep by $^3/_8$"-wide groove in the front and sides for the bottom. Sand your pieces and then assemble the drawers with nails and glue. Fit your drawers into the till. Finish-sand everything and cover the till with two coats of clear finish. Add a chain to the lid to prevent it from opening too far.

Build the Runners

The till rests on runners screwed into the inside of the large case. These runners are made by using your table saw to cut two rabbets in $1^1/_4$" pine (photo 6). Screw the runners to the inside of the case. Be sure you leave a couple inches of space above the top of the till to allow room for the saw holder.

Saw Holder

Make the saw holder by screwing strips of 1"-thick pine to the lid of the large case (photo 7). Position the strips for your own set of saws. You might want to cut rabbets or dadoes in the strips depending on your particular saws. I made the front face of the saw holder from pine and leftover walnut veneer. After cutting the panel to size, cut a $^1/_2$"×$^1/_2$" rabbet on all four edges. Miter and glue four strips of maple into the rabbet.

Screw the front face to the strips and cover the screw heads with caps. I cut my own diamond-shaped caps from some scrap maple. Stain the interior of the large case and lid. To make the inside look old and weathered, I first put down a coat of walnut oil stain and allowed that to dry, then applied a cherry gel stain. Then I covered the interior and saw holder with two coats of clear finish, sanding lightly between coats.

Even though the tool chest is made almost entirely of pine, it weighs quite a bit. In fact, when the chest is fully loaded, it takes two strong backs to move it. After lugging it around, it made me think that maybe this was the reason Benjamin Seaton decided to stay in England.

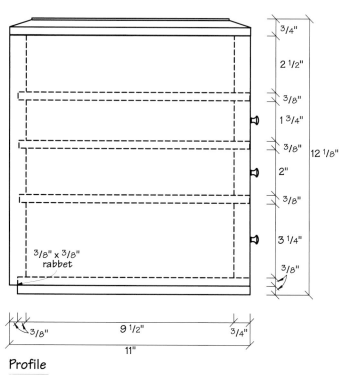

Schedule of Materials • Till Drawers

Drawer A (two drawers)

No.	Item	Dimensions T W L	Material
2	Drawer front	$3/4$" x $3\,1/4$" x $8\,3/4$"	Maple
4	Sides	$3/8$" x $3\,1/4$" x $9\,7/8$"	Pine
2	Back	$3/8$" x $2\,5/8$" x $8\,3/8$"	Pine
2	Bottom	$3/8$" x $8\,1/8$" x $9\,1/2$"	Plywood

Drawer B (one drawer)

No.	Item	Dimensions T W L	Material
1	Drawer front	$3/4$" x $3\,1/4$" x $13\,3/4$"	Maple
2	Sides	$3/8$" x $3\,1/4$" x $9\,7/8$"	Pine
1	Back	$3/8$" x $2\,5/8$" x $13\,3/8$"	Pine
1	Bottom	$3/8$" x $13\,1/8$" x $9\,1/2$"	Plywood

Drawer C (two drawers)

No.	Item	Dimensions T W L	Material
2	Drawer front	$3/4$" x 2" x 13"	Maple
4	Sides	$3/8$" x 2" x $9\,7/8$"	Pine
2	Back	$3/8$" x $1\,7/16$" x $12\,5/8$"	Pine
2	Bottom	$3/8$" x $12\,5/8$" x $9\,1/2$"	Plywood

Drawer D (one drawer)

No.	Item	Dimensions T W L	Material
1	Drawer front	$3/4$" x 2" x $5\,1/4$"	Maple
2	Sides	$3/8$" x 2" x $9\,7/8$"	Pine
1	Back	$3/8$" x $1\,7/16$" x $4\,7/8$"	Pine
1	Bottom	$3/8$" x $4\,7/8$" x $9\,1/2$"	Plywood

Drawer E (two drawers)

No.	Item	Dimensions T W L	Material
2	Drawer front	$3/4$" x $1\,3/4$" x $9\,1/2$"	Maple
4	Sides	$3/8$" x $1\,3/4$" x $9\,7/8$"	Pine
2	Back	$3/8$" x $1\,1/8$" x $8\,1/8$"	Pine
2	Bottom	$3/8$" x $8\,1/8$" x $9\,1/2$"	Plywood

Drawer F (one drawer)

No.	Item	Dimensions T W L	Material
1	Drawer front	$3/4$" x $1\,3/4$" x $12\,1/4$"	Maple
2	Sides	$3/8$" x $1\,3/4$" x $9\,7/8$"	Pine
1	Back	$3/8$" x $1\,1/8$" x $11\,7/8$"	Pine
1	Bottom	$3/8$" x $11\,7/8$" x $9\,1/2$"	Plywood

Profile

Tool Chest
Diagram of till with drawer dimensions
Scale 3" = 1'-0"

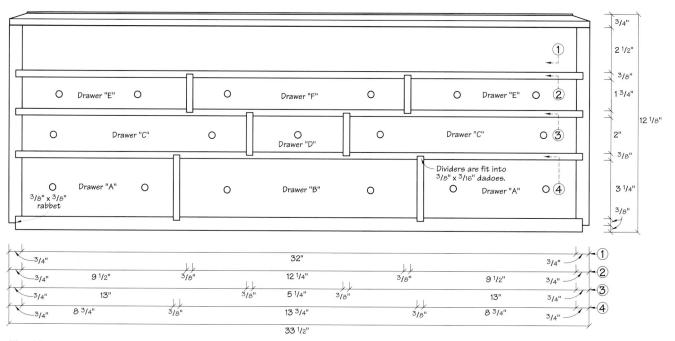

Elevation

Common Wood Defects

When purchasing wood for the Benjamin Seaton's Tool Chest project, or for any other project, be aware of these common wood defects.

Knot A dark whorl from a cross section of a branch. Knots weaken wood and affect appearance.

Bark Pockets Encased area of bark in board. Bark pockets reduce strength and lessen appearance.

Insect Damage Insects can cause holes in boards that reduce board strength.

Fungal Damage Fungi can stain wood. Called spalting, wood with advanced fungal decay may be weakened, and when cut, will release spores that can cause severe allergic reactions.

Check A separation between growth rings at the end of a board. Checks are common and lessen appearance, but do not weaken wood unless deep.

Shake A separation between growth rings that results in a slat coming loose from the face of the board.

Gum A sticky accumulation of resin that bleeds through finishes.

Pitch Pockets Pitch-filled spaces between grain layers. May bleed after board is milled; occasionally bleeds through finishes.

Machine Burn Blunt planer knives may burn the face of the board.

Machine Waves Incorrect planer speeds may create waves on the face of the wood. Boards with waves must be thinned again.

Bow An end-to-end warp along the face of the board. Bowed boards are fit for horizontal load-bearing if placed convex side up.

Cup An edge-to-edge warp across the face of the board. Cupped boards are fit for nonload-bearing use if placed convex side up or out.

Crook An end-to-end warp along the board edge. Fit for horizontal load-bearing if placed convex side up.

Twist A lop-sided or uneven warp. Wood is weakened, but twisted boards are fit for nonload-bearing use.

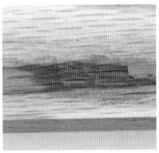

QUIET TIPS

PUT A MUFFLER ON IT • Your shop vacuum is a major source of noise. You can buy or make a muffler for the blower outlet port on the top of the machine. These are usually little more than plastic baffles that cut the roar down to size. The photo shows an inexpensive manufactured muffler that fits most vacuums with 2¼" exhaust ports. You can assemble your own using plastic plumbing pipe and an hour's worth of work.

NO DANCING ALLOWED • Keep a machine from doing the workshop rumba with hockey pucks. These hard rubber biscuits are available at any sporting goods store. Drill a hole through the center to accept a bolt and washer, and attach to the feet of the dancing machine.

BELT IT ONE • The rubber V-belts on your shop equipment are a major source of noise and vibration. It's because the belts aren't actually flexible enough to conform to the path they follow. Link belts solve this problem because they're much more flexible without any loss of power. They're typically sold by the foot and in a ½" width. You can find them at woodworking stores and in catalogs. You might also want to check local bearing supply houses (check your phone book).

TILE DOORS AND WALLS
Acoustical ceiling tile makes a great sound deadener. The pieces interlock, so with a bit of construction adhesive, it's a cinch to add a sound barrier to doors and walls shared with the house. You can cut them to fit with a utility knife, and they're offered in a variety of sizes and styles.

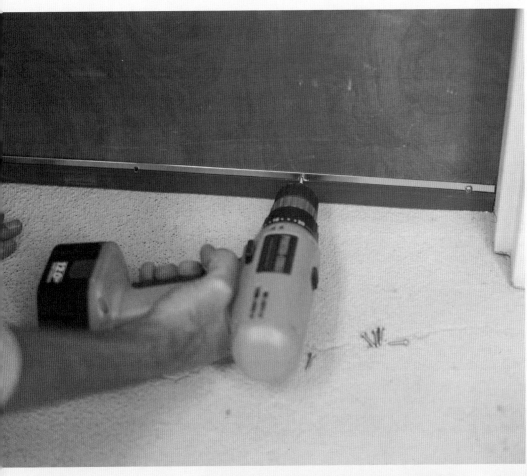

SWEEP NOISE AWAY • Most connecting doors in a home don't have a door sweep at their bottom, or if they do, it's worn away or flimsy. That little gap at the bottom of a door is a superhighway for sound transmission. So find a premium-quality door sweep at your favorite home center store and mount it to the door on the shop side.

CANCEL THE VIBES • If your power tools are mounted on bolt-together steel stands, congratulations on having created a new musical instrument. The machine's vibration plucks and twangs at all of those pieces of steel like an out-of-tune guitar. Here's a way to cancel the bad vibes. When you're assembling a new tool stand, squirt a dollop of clear silicone caulk at every bolted or screwed-together joint you encounter. For an existing tool stand, you'll have to do some disassembly, but the work will pay off in less noise in your shop.

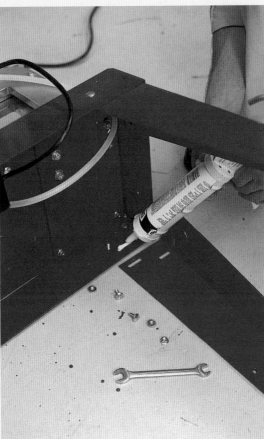

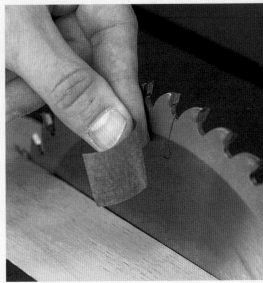

TAPE THOSE SAW BLADE SLITS • The blade manufacturers make table saw blades with cooling slits in them to allow the metal to expand and contract as it warms and cools. That's great for the blade, but it's hard on your ears because those slits cause a lot of noise in your shop. A cheap, simple noise-reducing fix that won't hurt the blade is to put tabs of masking tape over the slits; just keep it below the carbide-tooth level.

Bullet-proof
Bench

The first shop I worked in was run by a German cabinetmaker from the old school. Even though it was a commercial shop, things were done in the traditional way. We used modern power tools, but most of our work was performed on traditional European-style workbenches. These benches were made with a sturdy frame and a thick maple top. One twist was the cast-iron vises on the front and the end and a row of dog holes drilled in line with the dog on the tail vise. Until a couple of years ago, that bench was the best I'd used.

Then I got to use an actual nineteenth-century patternmaker's bench. It was a bit lower than I was used to. It was equipped with a patternmaker's vise made by the Emmert Company. The vise pivoted 90 degrees and rotated 360 degrees. It also had a small set of jaws on its bottom side for holding small parts. The wide jaws tapered to hold odd-sized objects. It was an excellent vise for just about any type of woodworking. Alas, the Emmert Company is long gone, and unless you find an old one of those cast-iron behemoths, you'll have to settle for a reproduction. Woodcraft has a nice Emmert reproduction (shown in the photo), and at $250, it costs roughly one-fifth of what actual patternmakers' vises are going for today.

For my bench, I wedded my two favorite benches — the bench in the photo is their firstborn. In addition to possessing the best traits of its parents, it has a few options that make it an original.

The bench has the versatility to perform many tasks. It has a row of dog holes for hand planing, routing and carving. There's a utilitarian tail vise on one end with the patternmaker's vise on the front.

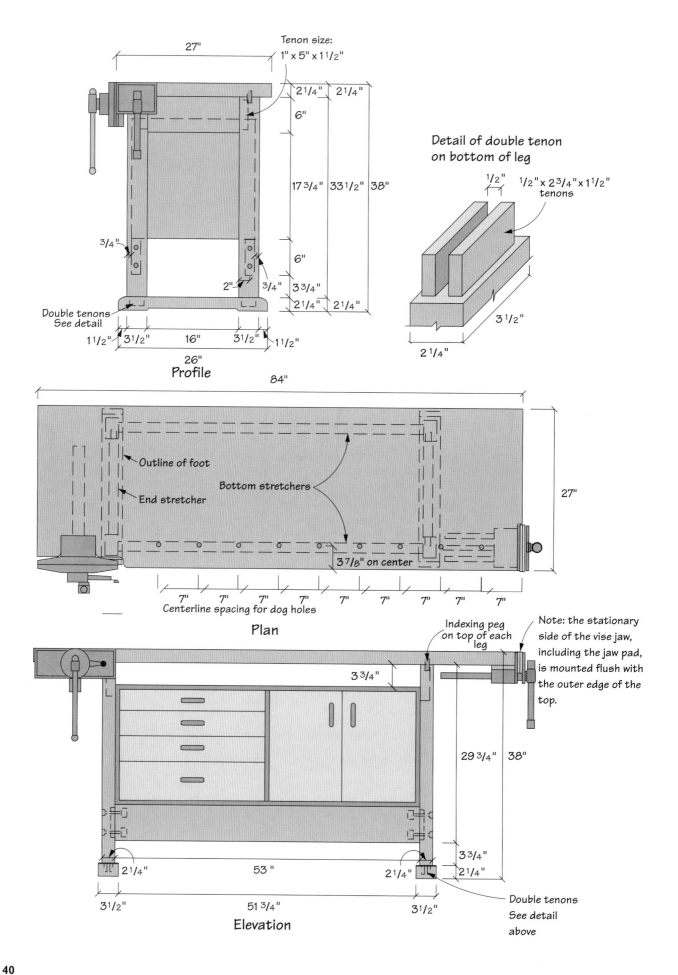

Tenon size:
1" x 5" x 1½"

27"

2¼"   2¼"

6"

17¾"   33½"   38"

6"

3¾"

2"   ¾"   2¼"   2¼"

¾"

Double tenons
See detail

1½"   3½"   16"   3½"   1½"

26"

Profile

Detail of double tenon
on bottom of leg

½"   ½" x 2¾" x 1½"
tenons

3½"

2¼"

84"

Outline of foot

End stretcher

Bottom stretchers

27"

3⅞" on center

7"   7"   7"   7"   7"   7"   7"   7"   7"

Centerline spacing for dog holes

Plan

Indexing peg
on top of each
leg

3¾"

Note: the stationary
side of the vise jaw,
including the jaw pad,
is mounted flush with
the outer edge of the
top.

29¾"   38"

3¾"

2¼"   53"   2¼"   2¼"

3½"   51¾"   3½"

Double tenons
See detail
above

Elevation

1 VISES AND DOGS • Some of the hardware I chose for my bench includes a Jorgensen tail vise, a patternmaker's vise, several dogs and hold-downs from Veritas Co. and the bolts for the legs.

A BULLET-RIDDLED BENCH

When you're dealing with heavy lumber, don't be surprised to find a few old bullets in the wood. Mills usually find these stray projectiles in thinner stock before they get to your lumberyard, but that's not always the case with wood this thick.

I found a few slugs in the 10/4 maple while I was resawing the wood for the top. The bullets appeared as a shiny glint on the wood's surface during a cut. I easily removed the metal with a chisel. The small slugs I found were most likely from a .22-caliber rifle, though I've found much larger ones in the past. I'd recommend keeping the bullets as a conversation piece so that when people ask you about your bench, you can tell them a "war story."

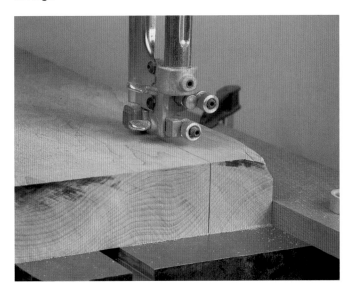

2 RIP YOUR PLANKS • Cut your maple planks into 2½" widths. The photo here shows the cuts being made on a band saw. I made a few cuts this way, and then I made the remainder of the cuts on the table saw. Either way, make sure you have a friend or a roller table to catch your work.

Schedule of Materials • Workbench

No.	Item	Dimensions T W L	Material
1	Top	2¼" x 27" x 84"	Maple
4	Legs	2¼" x 3½" x 35"	Maple
2	Feet	2¼" x 3½" x 26"	Maple
2	Front/Rear Stretchers	1½" x 6" x 54½"	Maple
2	End Stretchers	1⅝" x 6" x 19"	Maple

Choose Your Metal

Before you cut the first piece of wood, make sure you have all the hardware you need. This includes the vises, any dog hardware and the bolts for the knockdown base. Begin your bench by laying out the top to accommodate the vises. Measure the vises and the dogs to find the proper spacing they require to operate. Make sure the dogs don't interfere with vise operation. Next, determine what style of base you will use. My "apprentice" bench had four stout legs with upper and lower stretchers. The patternmaker's bench had sled feet, and the base was two end assemblies connected by two wide stretchers. This is the base I chose.

Make the Top

The top and much of the base was made from two large planks of 10/4 hard maple (about 80 board feet). The stretchers were made from laminated pieces of 4/4 maple that yielded material about 1⅝" thick (two boards 7"×14', about 16 bf). Lay out the rough cuts on the large planks and make your initial cross cuts.

After jointing an edge on each plank, rip the planks to about 2½" widths. The lumber that I bought was flat-sawn. What I accomplished by ripping was to turn the 2½" widths 90 degrees and glue them together, thereby creating a quartersawn top. This is a desirable feature because a quartersawn surface cuts down on cupping and warping.

Put the Pieces Back Together

Glue the top together in sections of 8"
or less in width. This makes it easier to
surface one side on an 8" jointer and
then plane to get a uniform thickness.
Then glue up two halves of the top; and
after cleaning these sections up, glue
the two halves together. For a little variety I added pieces of 4/4 maple into
the top for their decorative effect.
When you have the entire top glued together you can begin doing whatever
flattening is necessary. I have an old 24"
Stanley #7 corrugated jointer plane,
which worked perfectly for this process.

To cut the ends square, you could
use a very nice cabinetmaker's saw and
sliding table, but I am going to share a
simple, cheap method for squaring the
ends of large panels using a straightedge and a circular saw. I have a "Clam-
p'n Tool Guide," which is a straightedge
with small clamping jaws. The straightedge can be used to guide a circular
saw. Simply measure the distance from
the saw base edge to the blade and
mark that distance from your finish-cut
line on the top. (Do this with a framing
square.) Clamp the straightedge to the
top at the offset line and cut the top
square. You might have to take more
than one pass at different depths if your
saw isn't powerful enough to cut the entire thickness.

Next shape the top so your vises will
fit well. Both of the vises came with
complete instructions for installation on
the bench top. Some vises will require
routing in the top, others need buildup
(like my Jorgensen vise). Next come
the dog holes. I used bench dogs and
hold-downs from the Veritas Co. These
require a ¾" hole. In order to lay out
the holes properly, first measure the
maximum opening on your tail vise. In
my case, it was the Jorgensen. The
maximum opening was 9", so I laid out
the dog holes on 7" centers at 7" from
the dog on the vise. So unless your material is less than 7" in length it can
comfortably be clamped in this dog system. Next, make the holes in the top for
the dogs. The instructions for the Veritas bench dogs show how to rig a jig for
drilling those holes.

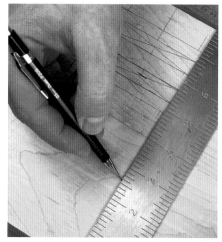

3 ASSEMBLE THE TOP Now that you have ripped your maple into strips, it's time to glue them back together. Use regular wood glue (no bis-cuits) and make sure the one side of the wooden strips that hasn't been squared is facing up. In addition to clamping the width of the top, I also clamped the ends to my gluing surface.

4 MAKE MORTISES • See the plans for the locations of the mortises on the legs and feet. If you don't have a mortising machine, use a drill press with a ½" bit and then clean out the waste with a chisel. No matter which machine you use, you will have to clamp your work to the table as you cut each hole. The mortises in the feet and for the top stretchers are 1½" deep; the mortises for the long bottom stretchers are ¾" deep.

Mortise the Legs and Feet

Your bench height should relate directly
to your height. I used the height of my
hip bone as a guide (about 38"). This is
a good height for me because it won't
cause undue back strain. First cut the
legs, feet and stretchers to length. Lay
out and cut the mortise and tenon
joints in the legs, feet and stretchers.
The short stretchers are mounted flush
to the inside of the leg assembly.

The front and back stretchers are
mounted ¾" back from the front and
back legs. This gives me room to add
accessories to my bench down the road.
To make the mortises, I used a hollow-
chisel mortising machine with a ½"
chisel bit, which makes nice, even mortise-and-tenon sizes.

For Sturdy Feet

Use a double tenon on the feet. This doubles the gluing surface and is a stout joint. Cut the tenons with a dado set, which yields a nice flat tenon. The stretchers' tenons are 1" thick. The double tenons for the feet are ½" wide each.

Making Things Fit

After cutting the mortises and tenons, some fitting may be required to get a snug fit. I used sharp ½" and ¾" chisels to clean out the mortises and used a shoulder plane to thin the tenons to size.

5 **TENONS •** Use a dado set in your table saw to cut the tenons. Your first pass should be the one that defines the shoulder. Then make several other passes to cut to the end. For extra strength, make the tenons that go into the feet double tenons. After you make the standard tenon, clamp the leg to a piece of wood as shown in the photo. Set your dado to cut ½" wide. The end result is two ½" tenons.

6 **CLEAN UP •** To clean up the mortises, use slicing cuts with your chisel as much as possible (left). Avoid the hammer. The only place you might have to use it is at the very end of the cut. Use a shoulder plane to trim the tenon cheeks (above). Make a few passes with the plane, then test your fit. Keep doing this until everything is snug.

Make Room for the Hardware

Before gluing the end assemblies together, drill the ⁷⁄₁₆" holes for the hardware. Use a drill press for the holes in the legs and a doweling jig for the holes in the stretchers.

Now make the square access holes in the stretchers with a ¾" Forstner bit, then square and clean up the holes with a sharp chisel. The ⅜" bolt will pass through the end of the legs, into the stretcher and end up here, which is where to attach the nut. Then cut the ⁷⁄₁₆" holes for the bolts in the ends of the stretchers.

Shape the Feet

To keep the ends of the feet from looking blocky, shape the top edge with a ⅞" roundover bit in your router table. Use a band saw to make a ⅜" cutout on the underside of the feet.

Assemble the Base

Bore the holes in the legs for the bolts. Then glue the end assemblies together. After the ends are dry, cleaned up and sanded, you can do a test assembly on the base.

With the bottom stretcher inserted into the leg mortise, use the ⁷⁄₁₆" bit to ream out the bolt passage. This will make your assembly easier. As you proceed to bolt the base together, you can

7 HARDWARE HOLES • After cutting the access holes in the side of the stretcher for the bolts (left), use a self-centering doweling jig to drill the holes for the bolts in the end of the stretchers (right).

set the nuts with some hot-melt glue. Dip your bolt ends into some petroleum jelly to keep them from sticking in the bolt, then squirt some hot-melt glue into the hole until the nut has been covered. This will make sure the nuts stay in the same place. When the glue has hardened, repeat the process on the other side of the base. Go ahead and disassemble the base and sand it. A coat of oil finish will seal the bench from humidity. Then reassemble the base.

8 FANCY FOOTWORK • If you don't have a ⅞" router bit to shape the top edges of the feet (left), cut a 45-degree bevel on the top with your table saw. Then ease the edges with sandpaper. To make the 16"-long cutout on the bottom of the sled feet, first make the relief cuts that define the ends. Then cut the bulk of the material out (right). And finally, clean up the ends.

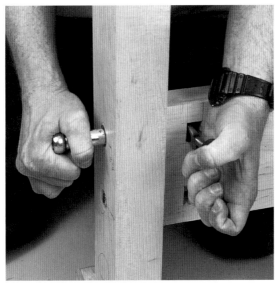

9 **TIME FOR THE BOLTS** • To make the holes in the legs for the bolts, first drill a 1" counterbore that is as deep as the head of the bolt. Then drill through the rest of the leg with a $^7/_{16}$" bit. Insert the stretcher into the mortise, put the bolt in, then tighten the bolt. I held the nut in place with needle-nose pliers.

TIPS ON THE TENONS

- When using a stacked dado to cut tenons, make the shoulder cut first. This will prevent tear-out occurring on the shoulder.
- When using circular saws to cut thick wood, take two or three passes at progressively deeper cuts. This will save your saw from burning out.
- A good way to drill the bolt holes is to drill the 1" counterbore to the depth of the bolt head and washer, then drill the bolt hole with a $^3/_8$" brad-point bit. Follow this with the $1^3/_{32}$" bit.
- When cutting tenons, cut them to be a snug fit, one that allows you to push it into the mortise using hand pressure only.

Place Your Top

With the bench's top upside down on the floor, position the base where you would like to attach it, and mark those locations. Turn the base over and mark the centers of the top of each leg. Drive a nail into the center of each leg. Leave about $^1/_4$" showing so you can remove the nail. Now set the top down on the base. Press down on the top to transfer the nail marks to the underside of the top. Drill $^3/_4$" holes into the top using the nail marks as centers. Do the same in the base. Glue a $^3/_4$" dowel into the top of each base leg and then attach the top. Don't glue the top to the dowels; the weight of the slab is enough to hold it in place.

When the glue is dry, install your vises. Then comes the one step you cannot skip. Put your mark on this bench, whether it's your signature or brand. Otherwise you'll be cheating future generations out of ever knowing its lineage.

10 **LAY OUT THE TOP** After you sand the top, put it facedown on two sawhorses. Then put the base on top and move it into position. Mark the location of the base on the bottom of the top. Then mark the location for the holes for the dowels and drill 1"-deep holes into the legs and top for the $^3/_4$" dowels that hold the top to the base.

All This and Storage, Too

The bench shown on the preceding pages stands on its own merits, but we decided tool storage space wouldn't be gilding the lily. The height of the cabinet allows the bench dogs to operate without obstruction, as well as adding storage for large flat items such as jigs.

First cut the carcase pieces to size according to the Schedule of Materials on the next page.

Cut the Rabbets

The rabbet joints are made on the table saw using a dado set and an auxiliary jig for the rip fence. Set the saw to remove ¾" (or whatever dimension your ¾" plywood is). Raise the dado set to ½" height and run both sides flat on the saw, rabbeting the top, bottom and back edges. The back edge of the top and bottom pieces should also be run at this time to form a rabbet for the ¾" back.

Reset the saw to cut a ¼" deep dado for the center partition. By setting the rip fence to cut 25¾" to the dado stack, the partition should be centered; but just to be on the safe side, make both dado cuts from the same end of the top and bottom (left or right).

Assembly is next. Glue and nail (or screw or staple) the center partition between the top and bottom. The partition should fit flush to the front edge, and flush to the inside edge of the rabbets in the top and bottom. If it's a tad wide, allow the extra on the front so it can be planed flush later. Attach the sides the same way, then drop the back in place housed by the four rabbets, and fasten.

1 RABBET JOINTS • The corners use a standard rabbet joint. Cut them using a dado stack on the table saw, leaving a ¼" x ¾" tab. The ¼" deep dado for the center partition can also be cut in the top and bottom at this time.

Tape the Ends

Cover the plywood edges with birch veneer tape that's sold in rolls with preglued, heat-sensitive adhesive. Cut the tape a little long for the piece and then apply it with a hot iron.

Press the Tape

When applied correctly, the cabinet looks like it's been assembled from solid lumber. First, apply the edges to the top and bottom pieces, trimming the ends of the tape flush to the inner edges of the sides. Next, apply the tape to the center partition, allowing the

tape to run over the top and bottom. Trim the tape flush to the previously taped edges. Tape the ends last. Use a wooden block to press the tape down.

Make the Drawers

With the case basically complete, it's time to build the drawers. Make your drawer boxes with simple joinery. A ¼" groove (set ¼" up from the bottom of the drawer sides and front) accepts the drawer bottom, which is nailed in place through the back.

All of the joints can be cut on the table saw. The four drawers shown in

2 IRON-ON TAPE • The veneer tape is applied using a standard household iron set for cotton. Keep the iron moving to avoid scorching.

3 PRESS YOUR WORK • While the adhesive is still warm and soft, use a block to keep the edges of the tape from curling while the glue cools and sets.

4 DRAWER CORNERS • A tongue and rabbet joint at each corner gives the drawer box lots of strength. The drawer face is then screwed to the box front.

our cabinet are all different sizes, providing a graduated depth that not only looks good but also provides for efficient use of the space. Feel free to make your drawer depths to suit your needs.

We used enamel-coated undermount slides for the drawers that required $3/8$" clearance on both sides of the drawer box. Many standard slides require a $1/2$" clearance per side, so adjust the drawer sizes in the Schedule of Materials if your slides don't use $3/8$" clearance. Otherwise, your drawers could be made the wrong size.

Extra Touches

The drawer faces and doors are dressed up by applying a simple molding made from $1/4$"×$7/8$" solid maple. Round over one edge with an $1/8$" radius bit in a router mounted in a table. These moldings are then miter-cut and glued to the plywood edges.

One piece of advice on the molding's miter cuts: We had difficulties with tearout on our saw, so we set up our disc sander and a slot-miter gauge set at a 45-degree angle. After cutting the mold-

ing to rough length, we finished the miter using the sander. To hang the doors, we used European-style hinges. The hinges you use are up to you. The cockbeading on the edges of the drawers and doors hides the plywood core and provides a nice detail to the project.

To keep the cabinet in place between the bench's stretchers, we attached four $1/2$"-thick blocks to the bottom of the cabinet.

These held the cabinet in place while still allowing it to be easily removed when necessary.

Schedule of Materials • Till Drawers

No.	Item	Dimensions T W L	Material
2	Top & bottom	$3/4$" x $21^1/2$" x $52^1/2$"	Birch Ply
2	Sides	$3/4$" x $21^1/2$" x 20"	Birch Ply
1	Partition	$3/4$" x $20^3/4$" x 19"	Birch Ply
1	Back	$3/4$" x $19^1/2$" x $52^1/2$"	Birch Ply
2	Doors	$3/4$" x $12^1/8$" x $17^7/8$"	Birch Ply
1	Drawer face*	$3/4$" x $24^3/4$" x $2^1/2$"	Birch Ply
1	Drawer face*	$3/4$" x $24^3/4$" x $3^1/2$"	Birch Ply
1	Drawer face*	$3/4$" x $24^3/4$" x 4"	Birch Ply
1	Drawer face*	$3/4$" x $24^3/4$" x $6^1/4$"	Birch Ply
2	Drawer sides	$1/2$" x 2" x $19^1/2$"	Birch Ply
2	Drawer sides	$1/2$" x 3" x $19^1/2$"	Birch Ply
2	Drawer sides	$1/2$" x $3^1/2$" x $19^1/2$"	Birch Ply
2	Drawer sides	$1/2$" x $5^3/4$" x $19^1/2$"	Birch Ply
1	Drawer front	$1/2$" x 2" x $24^1/8$"	Birch Ply
1	Drawer front	$1/2$" x 3" x $24^1/8$"	Birch Ply
1	Drawer front	$1/2$" x $3^1/2$" x $24^1/8$"	Birch Ply
1	Drawer front	$1/2$" x $5^3/4$" x $24^1/8$"	Birch Ply
1	Drawer back	$1/2$" x $1^1/2$" x $24^1/8$"	Birch Ply
1	Drawer back	$1/2$" x $2^1/2$" x $24^1/8$"	Birch Ply
1	Drawer back	$1/2$" x 3" x $24^1/8$"	Birch Ply
1	Drawer back	$1/2$" x $5^1/4$" x $24^1/8$"	Birch Ply
4	Drawer bottoms	$1/4$" x $19^1/4$" x $24^1/8$"	Birch Ply

*(Note: W is cross grain direction, L is long grain direction.)

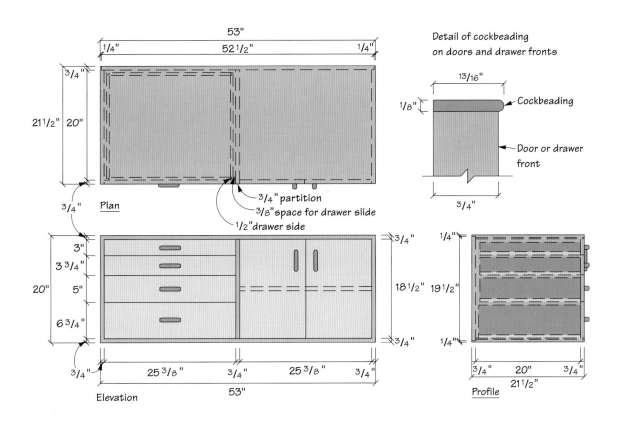

Detail of cockbeading on doors and drawer fronts

Plan

$3/4$" partition
$3/8$" space for drawer slide
$1/2$" drawer side

Elevation

Profile

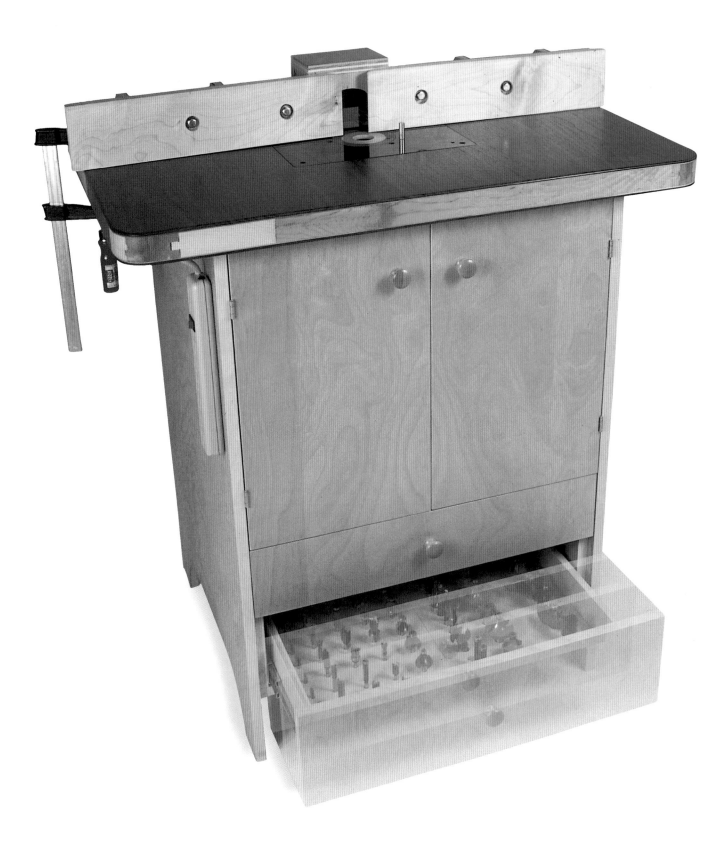

Practical Router Table

Numerous router table designs have been published recently in woodworking magazines. While most have interesting and arguably beneficial features, the cost-benefit analysis of the time required to build in all the bells and whistles might not make sense for many woodworkers. The table pictured here began as a simple and functional router table for our project shop here at Popular Woodworking.

Construction

Cut the pieces to size according to the schedule of materials. Apply iron-on birch veneer tape to the front edges of the two sides and to the front edges of the assembled drawer box. Assemble the drawer box section by nailing or screwing the box sides between the top and bottom. Nail or screw the drawer box between the two sides, allowing a 1" setback from the front edge of the sides. This will allow space for the inset doors and drawer faces.

The Top

Our top was constructed from a solid-core door. You could just as easily glue up a couple of pieces of ¾" plywood with a ¼" hardboard top to achieve a stable and smooth work surface. We purchased the table insert from Woodcraft's catalog [(800) 225-1153, www.woodcraft.com, item #16L73, $34.99]. It offers opening sizes from 4" to 1¼", which is changed easily with snap-in rings. The Deluxe Router Base plate is well worth the money. While you can make your own insert, this one offers a sturdy base with the variable-opening snap-in rings. Mounting instructions are included. Attach the top to the cabinet by first pre-drilling horizontal and vertical clearance holes in the cleats. Then screw the cleats to the top inside edge of each side, center the top, and screw up into the top through the cleats.

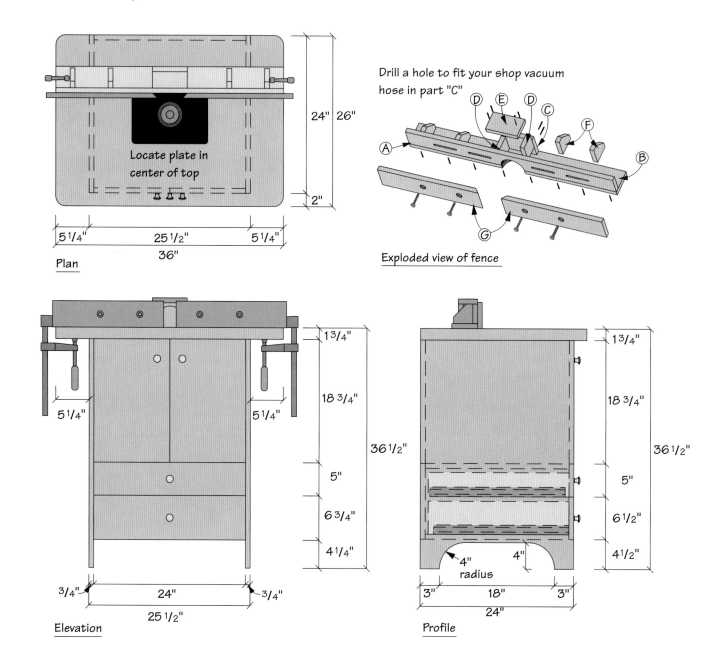

Plan

24" 26"

2"

5¹/₄" 25¹/₂" 5¹/₄"

36"

Drill a hole to fit your shop vacuum hose in part "C"

Exploded view of fence

Elevation

1³/₄"

18³/₄"

36¹/₂"

5"

6³/₄"

4¹/₄"

5¹/₄" 5¹/₄"

³/₄" 24" ³/₄"

25¹/₂"

Profile

1³/₄"

18³/₄"

36¹/₂"

5"

6¹/₂"

4¹/₂"

4" radius

4"

3" 18" 3"

24"

Locate plate in center of top

Doors and Drawers

The drawers are constructed by running ¹/₄"×¹/₄" rabbets on both ends of the front and back pieces. These form tenons that are then fit into ¹/₄"×¹/₄" grooves cut on the inside front-and-back edges of the sides. The bottoms are captured in ¹/₄"×¹/₄" grooves run ¹/₂" up from the bottom edge of the sides and front. The bottom is then nailed in place against the bottom edge of the drawer back. The drawers are mounted in the drawer box using full-extension slides to allow maximum benefit from

the space. We designated the bottom drawer as bit storage and cut a ³/₄" insert to lay in the drawer. We then drilled ¹/₂"- and ¹/₄"-diameter holes through the sub-base to allow us to store the bits upright. The doors and drawer faces have veneer tape applied to the top and side edges, leaving the bottom unfinished to allow for any final fitting. The drawer faces are screwed to the drawer fronts. The doors were hung using simple butt hinges to allow 180 degree opening for easier access to the router.

The Fence

The fence is a straightforward design. As shown in the diagram detail, the basic assembly of the fence starts by gluing the housing assembly together. The sides fit inside the top and rear, with the rear overlapping the top's back edge. A 2"-radius cutout is made at the center of both the base and front pieces to form the bit-clearance opening. The fence assembly is then glued together, with the front piece glued to the top surface of the base, and the housing glued into the corner formed by those two pieces. The

Schedule of Materials • Practical Router Table

No.	Item	Dimensions T W L	Material
2	Sides	$3/4$" x $23^{7}/8$" x 35"	Plywood
2	Box top & bottom	$3/4$" x $22^{1}/4$" x 24"	Plywood
2	Box sides	$3/4$" x 10" x $22^{1}/4$"	Plywood
1	Back	$3/4$" x 24" x $30^{1}/2$"	Plywood
1	Top	$1^{3}/4$" x 26" x 36"	Optional
4	Drawer sides	$1/2$" x $3^{1}/2$" x 22"	Plywood
2	Drawer fronts	$1/2$" x $3^{1}/2$" x 21"	Plywood
2	Drawer backs	$1/2$" x 3" x 21"	Plywood
1	Drawer face	$3/4$" x $23^{7}/8$" x $6^{1}/2$"	Plywood
1	Drawer face	$3/4$" x $23^{7}/8$" x 5"	Plywood
2	Doors	$3/4$" x $11^{7}/8$" x $18^{11}/16$"	Plywood
2	Drawer bottoms	$1/4$" x $21^{1}/32$" x $21^{3}/4$"	Plywood
2	Cleats	$3/4$" x 1" x 21"	Poplar

Schedule of Materials • Router Fence

No.	Ltr.	Item	Dimensions T W L	Material
1	A	Front	$3/4$" x 3" x 36"	Plywood
1	B	Base	$3/4$" x 4" x 36"	Plywood
1	C	Housing rear	$3/4$" x $3^{3}/4$" x $5^{1}/2$"	Plywood
2	D	Housing sides	$3/4$" x $2^{1}/2$" x 3"	Plywood
1	E	Housing top	$3/4$" x $3^{1}/4$" x $5^{1}/2$"	Plywood
4	F	Braces	$3/4$" x 3" x 3"	Plywood
2	G	Fence faces	$3/4$" x 4" x $17^{1}/2$"	Maple

Depending on your preference, the fence can be held in place simply using a clamp on each end (left), or the base piece can be extended 4" in length to add a homemade C-clamp (above). A simple threaded rod with a handle on one end and a nut on the other secures the fence to the table.

braces are then glued in place with the innermost brace spaced $5^{3}/8$" from the housing side and the outermost brace spaced $5^{3}/8$" from the first brace. The fence assembly should be glued and clamped to a straight surface to form a straight and square fence. The fence faces are maple with a 45 degree bevel cut on each inside edge to allow the maximum bit clearance and minimum throat opening. A $1/8$"x$1/8$" rabbet is cut on the front bottom edge to allow dust clearance. The faces are mounted with two bolts each through two 4"-long hor-izontal slots in the front. This allows the faces to slide left-to-right to expose only as much of the bit as necessary. The fence can be mounted in a couple of ways, which are detailed in the photos.

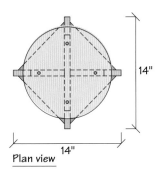

14"

14"

Plan view

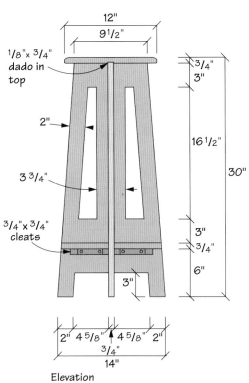

12"

9 1/2"

1/8" x 3/4" dado in top

2"

3 3/4"

3/4" x 3/4" cleats

3/4"

3"

16 1/2"

3"

3/4"

6"

30"

3"

2"   4 5/8"   4 5/8"   2"
3/4"
14"

Elevation

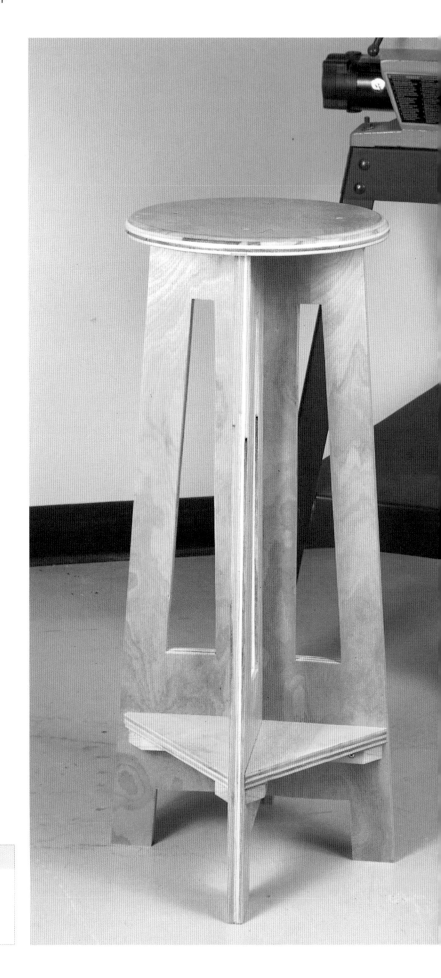

Schedule of Materials • Shop Stool

No.	Item	Dimensions T W L	Material
2	Legs	3/4" x 14" x 29 3/8"	Plywood
4	Braces	3/4" x 6" x 6"	Plywood
1	Top	3/4" x 12" x 12"	Plywood
8	Cleats	3/4" x 3/4" x 5"	Poplar

Shop
Stool

This stool is the perfect accessory for your workbench and takes just a few hours to build. You can make this stool at the height shown or as low or tall as you like. The height of this one is perfect for sitting at the scroll saw and other benchtop tools.

Construction

Cut the plywood and poplar according to the schedule of materials. Lay out the pattern for the two leg pieces. They are 14" wide at the bottom and 9½" wide at the top. Before cutting the two tapered legs, adjust a dado set to the thickness of the plywood and cut half-lap or egg-crate joints in the legs (see drawing of the legs before assembly). When done, cut the leg tapers. Using the same dado setup, cut two ⅛"-deep channels in the seat that intersect at the center. With a band saw or jigsaw, cut the seat into a circular shape. Then

use a ⅜" roundover bit in your router on the top edge of the seat. To make the footrest braces, cut two pieces of scrap plywood into 6" squares. Then cut both pieces corner to corner, creating four triangles. On the leg pieces, cut out the bottom edges to create the feet. Then make the elongated triangular cutouts. Assemble the two leg pieces.

Assembly

Lay out the location for the poplar cleats that hold the triangular braces. Taller people will be comfortable with the braces about 6" off the floor. Shorter folks will like the braces higher. If you raise the braces, you might have to make them a little smaller. Attach the cleats to the legs with 1¼" screws. Then screw the braces to the cleats. Attach the seat to the base assembly with four screws. Finish your stool as desired.

Schedule of Materials • Adjustable Sawhorse

No.	Item	Dimensions T W L	Material
8	Legs	1³⁄₄" x 3¹⁄₂" x 21⁵⁄₈"	Poplar
2	Cross braces	1³⁄₄" x 3¹⁄₂" x 30"	Poplar
4	Brace plates	¹⁄₂" x 8" x 10"	Plywood
4	Riser sides	³⁄₄" x 29" x 11"	MDF
4	Ends	³⁄₄" x 1³⁄₄" x 8"	MDF
2	Bottoms	³⁄₄" x 1³⁄₄" x 27¹⁄₂"	MDF
2	Riser tops	³⁄₄" x 3¹⁄₄" x 29"	MDF
2	Index pins	³⁄₄" dia. x 4"	Oak dowel

Adjustable
Sawhorse

A level worktable will help you assemble your projects, both plumb and square. The adjustable height mechanism shown in the diagram easily levels at four points using simple T-nuts and cap screws.

To begin, cut the sawhorse and riser parts. We used 8/4 poplar for the legs and cross brace and ¾" birch veneer MDF for the risers. The height of the horses alone is good for working on

cabinets. The addition of the riser provides a good height for routing, sanding and other flat work.

A band saw is the safest tool for making angle cuts (diagram) on the legs. A table saw can be used, but great care is needed for safety.

Using a 1" spade bit, drill and countersink for the heads, nuts and washers of the ⅜" machine bolts that secure the legs to the cross brace. Now lay two

legs on edge on two 1½" strips to locate the legs the appropriate distance in from the end of the cross brace. Stand the cross brace vertically and place it into the notches of the two legs, then clamp the assembly together and check for square.

Next, drill a ¼" pilot hole through the center of the previously made clearance hole. Then redrill using a ⁷⁄₁₆" bit and bolt the assembly together. Repeat the process with the other end. Lastly, attach the leg brace support plates with screws and glue.

Lay out, cut and radius the handholds on the sides of the riser boxes, then assemble using butt joints, screws and glue. Attach the top piece, then cut the notches in the bottom of the riser and set the unit on the horse.

Next, drill a ¾" hole through the overhang on the riser and the center of the cross brace for the dowel indexing pin.

On the top edge of the cross brace and the top of the riser box, mark 24" centers in the middle of each piece. Drill two ⁷⁄₈"×⅛" deep holes with a Forstner or spade bit. Then place a punch-out from a metal electrical box into each hole. The disk has about a ⁷⁄₈" diameter and will allow the cap screws in the worktop to rest on a hard surface. Now install T-nuts and cap screws into the top (a 1¾" solid-core door cut to size works well) on 24" centers so the screws line up with the inserts.

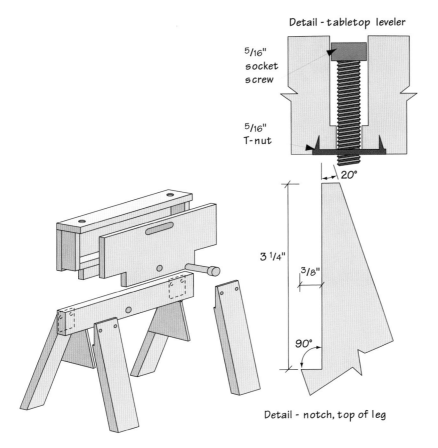

Detail - tabletop leveler

5/16" socket screw

5/16" T-nut

20°

3 1/4"

3/8"

90°

Detail - notch, top of leg

GLUE & CLAMP TIPS

BETTER LIDS • Use screw-on electrical wire nuts to replace the easy-to-lose caps on glues, caulks and other products. Besides being more visible, they come in a variety of sizes and colors, and the wings allow you to put some 'oomph' into unscrewing a sticky cap.

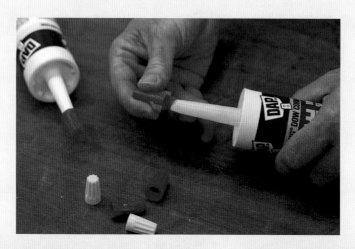

CHISEL, DON'T WIPE • A lot of books and magazines advise you to use a damp rag to wipe away wood glue that oozes out. The problem is that, unless you're hugely careful, you can actually spread the glue around in the course of wiping it up, creating an even bigger mess and staining problem. A technique we think is better is to let the glue dry for just a bit — typically about 15 minutes — and then scrape it away with a chisel.

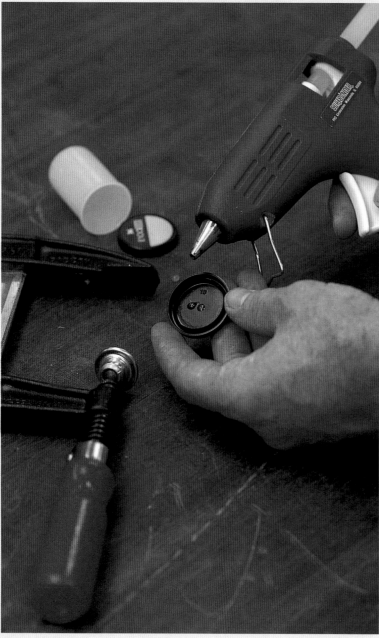

SOFT CLAMP JAWS ON THE CHEAP
Keep your clamps and vise from damaging the work surface by using a hot-melt glue gun to attach plastic film container lids or pieces of leather to the jaws.

PIPE CLAMP GLUE-UP JIG
Build this simple frame to hold your pipe clamps in alignment when gluing up projects. You'll be able to clamp pieces straight and true and not have to jiggle things around to get everything lined up. Build the frame by first laying out and drilling the hole centers to match your pipes, then rip the piece down the middle of the holes. Then make two end pieces in the same manner, and assemble with glue and screws.

ODDBALL GLUING JOBS • The hardest part of many small glue and fix-it jobs is simply figuring out how to hold the dang thing in place. Our answer? Go play in the sandbox. Fill a small container with a layer of sand, then place the oddball part that's been frustrating you in the sand, working it around until you have it in the right position. Now glue away. You can also fill a few small plastic freezer bags with sand to serve as weights or additional propping.

DIP YOUR BISCUITS • As much as we like biscuit joiners and the little wafers that help make good, tight joints, actually gluing them up is a bit of a pain if you've got a lot. So do what we've learned to do. Fill a small container with wood glue, thinning it slightly with water. Then just dip the biscuit into the glue like you're doing the dip-n-chip routine at a party, and put it into its slot. This is a real time-saver when you've got a lot of biscuits to install.

Drill Press
Table

Despite the fact that your drill press is designed mostly for poking holes in sheet metal, it has many uses in a woodshop. It's a mortiser and a spindle sander, it bores huge holes, and — of course — it drills holes at perfect right angles to the table. Because the table on most drill presses is designed for metalworking, it's hardly suited for these tasks. So I built this add-on table with features that will turn your drill press into a far friendlier machine:

• First, a fence that slides forward and backward as well as left and right on either side of the quill. This last feature also uses the drill press's tilting-table feature with the auxiliary table for angled drilling.

• Built-in stops (both left and right) that attach to the fence for repetitive procedures such as doweling or chain drilling for mortises.

• Hold-downs that can be used on the fence or on the table for any procedure.

The sizes given in the schedule of materials are for a 14" drill press, with the center falling 9" from the rear edge of the table, with a 2" notch in the back to straddle the column. Adjust the center location and overall size of the table to match your particular machine.

Start With the Base-ics

The base platform for the table is made from ¾" plywood, which should be void-free. Again, adjust the size as necessary to fit your drill press. First, you need to get the table ready for the T-slot track, which is what holds the fence and hold-downs in place. Start by locating the four recessed holes that allow the T-slot mechanism to slip into the track without disassembling the mechanism. Each hole is 1½" in diameter and ⅜" deep.

Next, locate the grooves in the center of the holes and use a router with a ¾"-wide straight bit to cut the grooves to a ⅜" depth. The T-slot track should fit into the grooves with the top surface just below that of the plywood table. The grooves should be as parallel as possible to one another to allow smooth movement of the fence.

Replaceable Center

Now cut the hole for the 4"×4" replaceable insert. First locate and mark the position centered on your table, then mark in from that line by ⅜" to locate your cutting line. Drill clearance holes in two corners of the square, then use a jigsaw to cut out the center piece. Next, determine the thickness of the material you will use for your insert (the ⅜"-thick

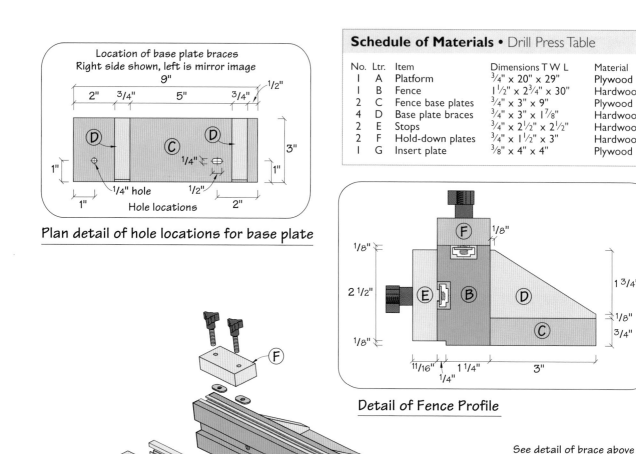

Location of base plate braces
Right side shown, left is mirror image

Plan detail of hole locations for base plate

Schedule of Materials • Drill Press Table

No.	Ltr.	Item	Dimensions T W L	Material
1	A	Platform	¾" × 20" × 29"	Plywood
1	B	Fence	1½" × 2¾" × 30"	Hardwood
2	C	Fence base plates	¾" × 3" × 9"	Plywood
4	D	Base plate braces	¾" × 3" × 1⅞"	Hardwood
2	E	Stops	¾" × 2½" × 2½"	Hardwood
2	F	Hold-down plates	¾" × 1½" × 3"	Hardwood
1	G	Insert plate	⅜" × 4" × 4"	Plywood

Detail of Fence Profile

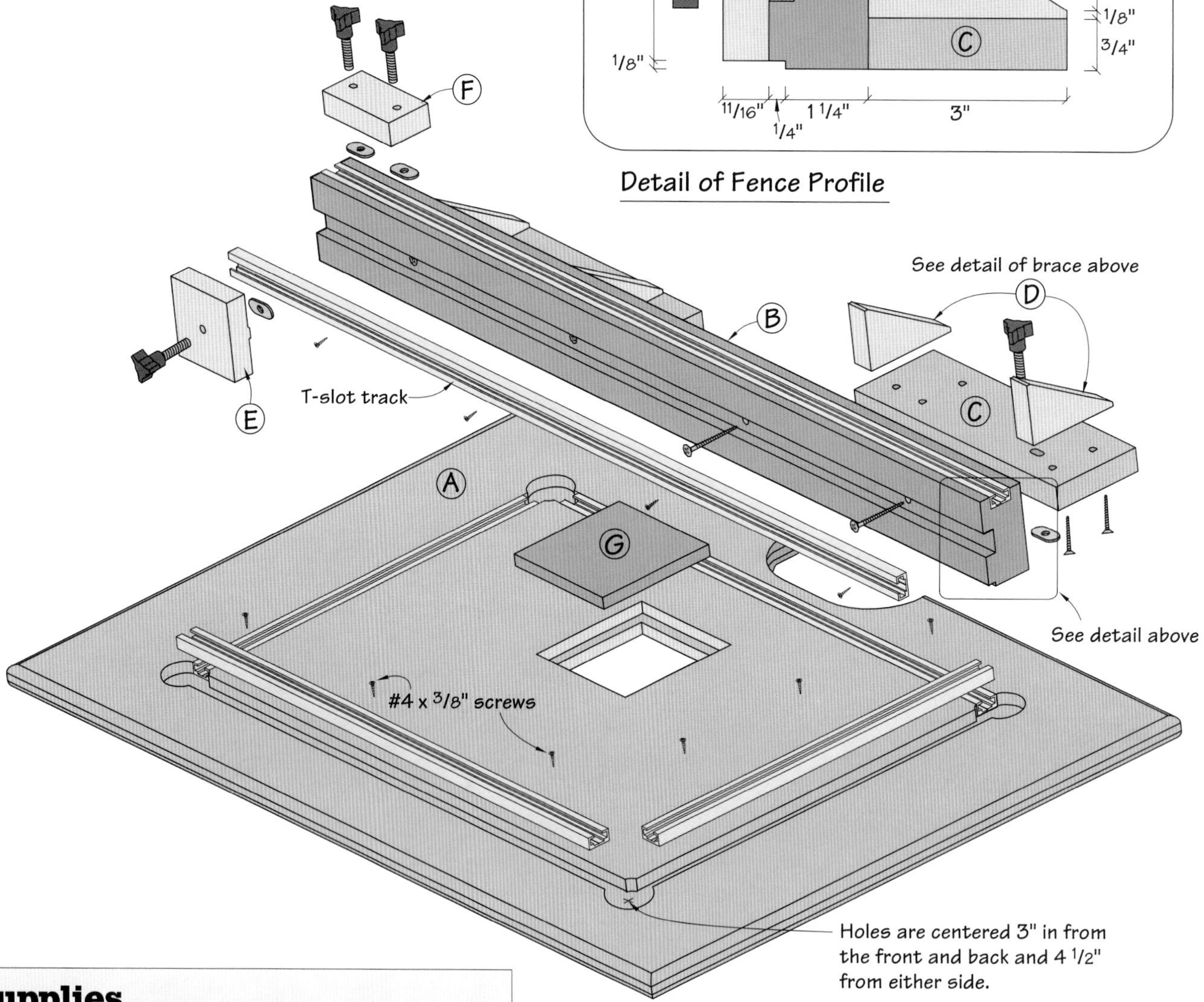

See detail of brace above

See detail above

T-slot track

#4 × ³⁄₈" screws

Holes are centered 3" in from
the front and back and 4 ¹⁄₂"
from either side.

Supplies

From Lee Valley, 800-871-8158, www.leevalley.com:
- 2- De-Sta-Co Clamps - $14.50 ea. Item #88F05.02
- 6- 24" T-Slot Tracks - $4.95 ea. Item #12K7901
- 8- 1⅛" 3-Wing Knobs - $6 for 10. Item #00M5102
- 8- T-Nuts - $1.15 for 10. Item #05J2115

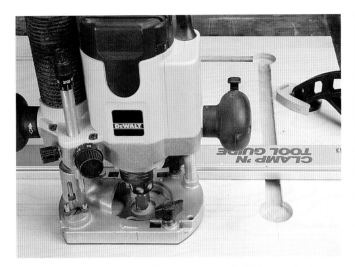

1 ROUT THE GROOVE • The grooves for the T-slot track allow the fence to be used left-to-right and front-to-back on the table to take advantage of the built-in tilting feature of the existing table.

2 RABBET FOR THE INSERT • After cutting the hole with a jigsaw, the opening is rabbeted using a bearing-piloted router bit. Then chisel the corners square and fit the replaceable center tightly into the rabbet. Make a couple extras.

Baltic birch we used is actually metric and shy of ⅜") and set a ⅜" piloted rabbeting bit in a router to a height to hold the insert flush to the top surface of the table.

While your jigsaw is still out, locate, mark and cut out the notch in the back of the table. This allows the table to move closer to the drill press's post and to tilt without interference.

As a final friendly touch on the table, I used a ⅜" roundover bit in my router to soften all the edges on the table, both top and bottom. You'll get fewer splinters if you do this.

Milling the Fence
The fence is the heart of the table, and the wood should be chosen for durability and straightness. Quartersawn hardwood, carefully surfaced and planed, will do nicely. After cutting the fence to size, use a dado stack to mill two ⅜"-deep by ¾"-wide grooves in the fence. The first is centered on the top surface of the fence, and as in the grooves in the base platform, a piece of T-slot track should be used to confirm that the groove is deep enough to allow the track to fit just below the surface of the wood. The second groove is then cut centered on the face of the fence. One other bit of table saw work is the ⅛"×¼"-wide rabbet cut on the inside bottom edge of the fence. This rabbet allows dust and

debris to be pushed into the rabbet, so your work will fit against the fence.

One option that I considered was adding an indexing tape measure on the fence. Every time the table is moved, the tape would need to be readjusted to zero, and for the infrequent use the tape would see, I decided against it. A stick-on tape can easily be added to the fence face if that's more to your personal taste and needs.

Fence Support Braces
Unlike the fence on a router table, the fence on a drill press table won't see a lot of lateral pressure. So the main purpose of the braces is to hold the fence square to the table at the drilling point. In my case, I've also given the braces the job of mounting the fence to the table.

Start by cutting the two base plates and the four braces to size. The braces are triangles with the bottom edge 3" long and the adjoining right-angle edge 1⅞" long. The third side is determined by simply connecting the corners. Locate the braces on the base plates according to the diagrams and predrill and countersink ³⁄₁₆"-diameter holes in the base plates to attach the braces to the plates.

To mount the support braces to the fence, again refer to the diagrams to locate the proper spacing on the fence.

Then drill and countersink screw holes through the face groove in the fence. Clamp the brace to the fence and screw the brace in place.

With the braces attached to the fence, use the T-slot fastener locations on the diagrams as a starting point for drilling the holes in the base plates, but check the location against your table for the best fit. Two holes are drilled in each plate to allow the fence to be moved to the perpendicular position (either to the right or left of the quill), by simply relocating one of the T-slot fasteners. Check each hole in relationship to that position.

Attaching the Track
Assuming you purchased the 24" lengths of track listed in the schedule of materials, you should be able to cut the tracks for the table first, leaving falloff that can be added to the two remaining full-length tracks to give you the necessary 30" lengths of track for the fence. When attaching the track, first drill a pilot hole in the center of the track (a groove is provided in the track to simplify that location), then use a countersink to widen the hole to accommodate a no. 4×⅝" flathead screw. Keeping the screws as flush as possible to the inner surface of the track will make the stops and hold-downs move much easier.

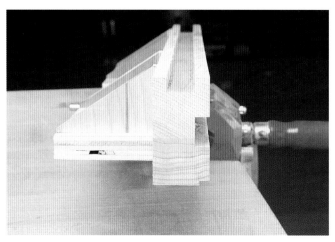

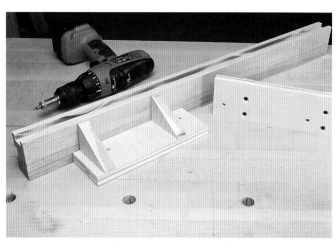

3 ROCK SOLID • The fence is made of a sturdy, stable hardwood. Cut a groove the length of the top and face of the fence. The grooves support T-slot tracks, which can be used for stops, hold-downs and other accessories.

4 FENCE BRACES • The fence is supported by two simple brackets screwed to the rear of the fence. The location of the triangular braces is important to the track orientation, so follow the diagrams carefully for location.

Finishing Touches

Stops and hold-downs designed for use in T-slot tracks make the drill press most useful. The stops are simply square blocks of wood with one side milled to leave an indexing strip that fits into the slot on the T-slot track. By using the saw to cut tall but narrow rabbets on two edges of each block, the stops are completed fairly easily. For safety, run the rabbet on a longer 2½"-wide piece of wood, then cut the stops to square afterwards. The T-slot fasteners are simply inserted into a ¼" hole drilled in the center of each stop block.

The hold-downs are blocks of wood with De-Sta-Co clamps mounted to the top. Each block is drilled for two T-slot fasteners, one on either end. Then the clamp is screwed to the top surface of the block. While the De-Sta-Cos are good for this application, they aren't as versatile as I wanted. I replaced the threaded-rod plunger with longer all-thread (¼"×36) to provide maximum benefit from the clamps. The rubber tip of the plunger is important to the function of the clamp, and if you can manage to reuse the existing tip, it's very helpful. If not, I found rubber stoppers in a variety of sizes in the local Sears hardware store. After carefully drilling a ¼"-diameter hole two-thirds of the way into the stopper, I was able to screw it onto the rod with little difficulty.

Attaching and Personalizing

The table should attach easily to your existing drill press table using four lag bolts countersunk flush into the surface of the auxiliary table. Once it's attached, you should find that the auxiliary table overhangs the metal table quite a bit. One personalized touch I want to suggest is adding small drawers to the underside of the table to store bits, wrenches and chuck keys.

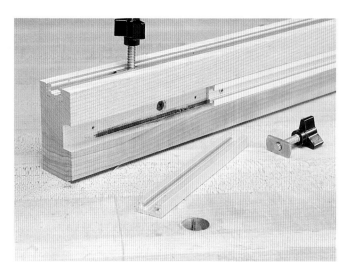

5 LAYING TRACKS • Install the T-slot tracks in the grooves with flathead screws countersunk into the track. The braces are attached to the fence by screwing through the face groove prior to attaching the T-slot track.

6 HOLD IT • The hold-downs and stops are made from ¾" hardwood. To make the guide to hold the stops square to the fence, cut a ¹⁄₁₆" x 1⅛" rabbet on both sides of the inside face.

HOOK HOLDER • Peg-Board hooks tend to fall out when an item is removed. There are all kinds of fancy solutions and screw-in hooks, but a hot-melt glue gun offers the fastest fix for this particular aggravation. Use the glue gun to put a dab or two of glue on the part of the hook that rests on top of the Peg-Board. Hold it in place until the glue sets — a few seconds. Hook in the wrong place? Use a heat gun or soldering iron for a few seconds to soften the glue.

EXCITING PEG-BOARD • Peg-Board doesn't have to be the same boring dirt brown. Much as we love the stuff in our shop, it's a really boring color. So dress it up with bright colors either before or after it goes up on your workshop walls. We like to use different colors just for eye appeal, but you could also arrange your tools, jigs and miscellaneous hardware according to color.

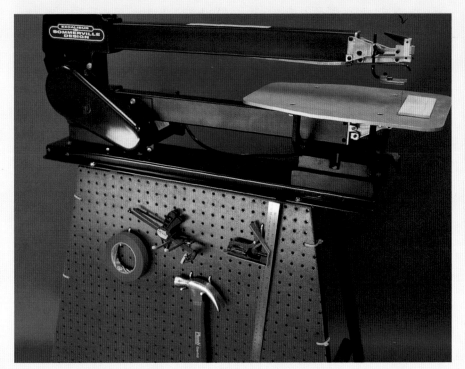

MOLDY GOLDIE • This is one of the oldest tricks in the workshop book, but it bears repeating. Anytime you find yourself in a nailing situation where you can't afford to have the hammer slip, use a scrap of Peg-Board to protect the surface. Just slip it over the nail and pound away.

PUT IT EVERYWHERE • The open sides of any tool stand give you a great place to store spare blades, adjustment tools, accessories and even the operating manual. Just cut pieces of Peg-Board to fit. You can attach the Peg-Board either by drilling holes in the stand and using bolts and nuts, or with plastic zip ties.

Five Shop Helpers

Sheet Goods Mover/Lifter

Let's face it, 4×8 sheets are a pain to handle. This simple and easy-to-make helper is just the answer for moving and lifting the materials (the offset arm will save your knuckles). Cut the parts, then glue the two base pieces together to make a piece 1½" thick. Glue the stiffener plate to the body plate and attach the angle iron with 1¼" drywall screws.

Assemble the rest of the project using glue and screws. When mounting the casters, make sure they are parallel with each other so the third hand will track in a straight line. After attaching the nonslip tape to the angle iron, you're ready to start saving your arms and back. For added strength holding the angle iron in place, use screws and polyurethane glue.

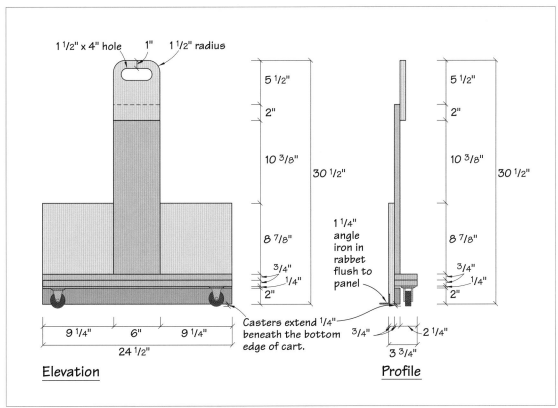

1 ½" x 4" hole   1"   1 ½" radius

5 ½"
2"
10 ³/₈"
30 ½"
8 ⁷/₈"
¾"
¼"
2"

1 ¼" angle iron in rabbet flush to panel

5 ½"
2"
10 ³/₈"
30 ½"
8 ⁷/₈"
¾"
¼"
2"

9 ¼"   6"   9 ¼"
24 ½"

Casters extend ¼" beneath the bottom edge of cart.

¾"   2 ¼"
3 ¾"

Elevation

Profile

Folding Sawhorse

This heavy-duty sawhorse is tough enough for any task, yet it easily folds up for storage. Lay out all the parts and cut them to size with a circular saw or jigsaw (one sheet of plywood will yield all the parts). Glue the stiffener pieces in place and lay both leg assemblies with the inside of the legs facing up on a flat work surface. Screw the continuous hinge into place. Put blocks on the workbench to keep the legs from spreading apart and stand the sawhorse up. Screw the hanger bolts in place and attach the arms. The top beam is two pieces of plywood glued together to make it 1½" thick. It's attached with two butt hinges and held tight for use with two gate hooks. Unhook the hooks, unlatch the arms and swing them out of the way, and the whole horse folds up to be led quietly to its corral. Need to make a lighter-duty version? Eliminate the stiffener pieces and enlarge the cutout on the legs.

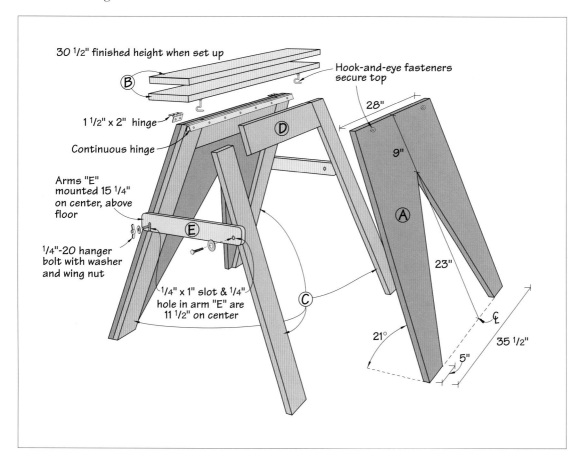

30 ½" finished height when set up

Hook-and-eye fasteners secure top

1 ½" x 2" hinge

Continuous hinge

Arms "E" mounted 15 ¼" on center, above floor

¼"-20 hanger bolt with washer and wing nut

¼" x 1" slot & ¼" hole in arm "E" are 11 ½" on center

28"

9"

23"

21°

5"

35 ½"

Scrap Wood Storage Bin

Any woodworker knows that large pieces of wood become smaller as your project progresses. These scraps usually end up on the floor, kicked under the bench, or tossed into the fireplace. This storage bin can help organize and keep your valuable scraps where you can retrieve them fast. Materials needed are a sheet of ¾" plywood, four casters, some screws and wood glue. Begin by cutting out all parts. Lay out the angle on the ends using a straightedge and cut out with a circular saw. Use glue and 2" drywall screws to assemble. Add the blocking to the bottom of the bin and use 1¼" drywall screws to attach the casters. Round over the sharp edges with sandpaper and you're ready to roll.

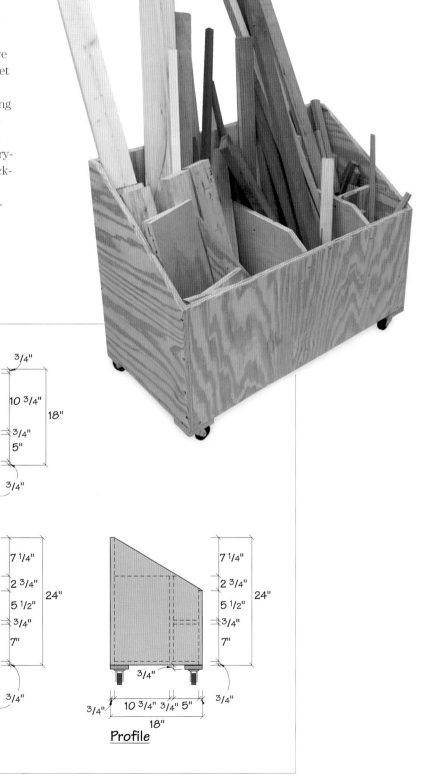

Plan

3/4"
10 3/4"
18"
3/4"
5"
3 ½"
Raised bottom
3/4"   16"   3/4"   10"   3/4"   7"   3/4"
36"

Elevation

7 1/4"
2 3/4"
5 1/2"
24"
3/4"
7"
3/4"
3/4"   16"   3/4"   10"   3/4"   7"   3/4"
36"

Profile

7 1/4"
2 3/4"
5 1/2"
24"
3/4"
7"
3/4"
3/4"   10 3/4"   3/4"   5"   3/4"
18"

Mobile Storage Cart

If your shop is small and space is at a premium (sound familiar?), you need this mobile storage cart. Only 47" long and 13" wide, the short wheelbase makes it easy to move. With one set of fixed casters and one set of movable casters, it can be easily steered around corners. This cart is made from one sheet of ¾" plywood and four casters. Start building your cart by crosscutting the 4×8 sheet in half to make it easier to handle, and then cut all the pieces. Lay out the angles on the end

pieces and cut with a circular saw using a straightedge clamped along the lines as a guide. Assemble using glue and 2" drywall screws. Attach the casters with 1¼" drywall screws making sure the fixed casters are both on the same end of the cart. If storage for full-size materials is going to be for an extended period, consider attaching three 8'-long 2×4s (make sure they are very straight) across the length of the rack to provide added support.

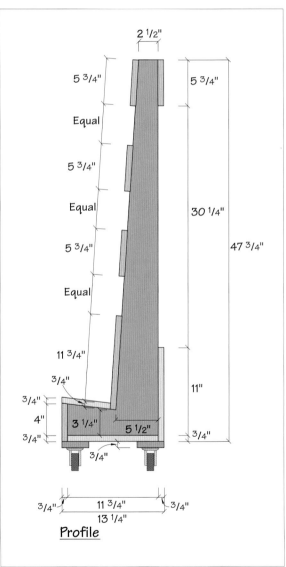

Profile

Table Saw Push Sticks

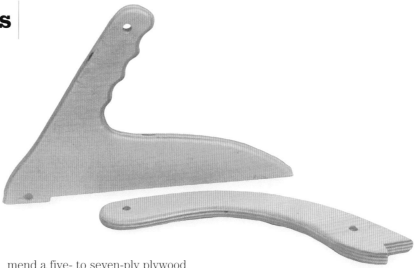

One inexpensive safety item that should never be out of reach is a push stick for your table saw. Though not every woodworker will agree on design (we didn't completely agree in the PW shop), two designs can be promoted as better than most.

The very recognizable "bird mouth" push stick (diagram) is frequently offered as a pattern or as an actual push stick by many saw manufacturers. The basic design works well to keep your hands above and behind the blade during most operations. The angle of the mouth is cut a little more than 90 degrees to allow easy seating against the materials being cut. It's most useful when cutting long, narrow strips, say 2"-wide by 48" or longer. With little concern of the workpiece being lifted by the blade's rotation, or binding, front-end pressure isn't essential.

For wide, short pieces of material, the second "shoe" design (diagram) offers reliable rear support, a sturdy handle for maintaining good control and grip, and an extended shoe area that supplies downward pressure against the front of the piece to protect against lifting.

Both designs should be made from sturdy ½" or ¾" material. We recom-

mend a five- to seven-ply plywood material instead of solid wood.

Once you have the basic design, individual preferences come into play, so you may want to fine-tune to meet your needs (and grip). We rounded over all of the edges (except for those that contact the wood) for comfort when gripping. Another feature we wouldn't do away with is the hole in the handle. If your push stick is hanging next to your saw where it belongs, you won't have an excuse not to use it.

While you're making one, make two or three of the same design. It's a tool, not furniture, and it may get cut up during some applications ... and better the stick than your hand. Plus, it never hurts to always have a spare lying around.

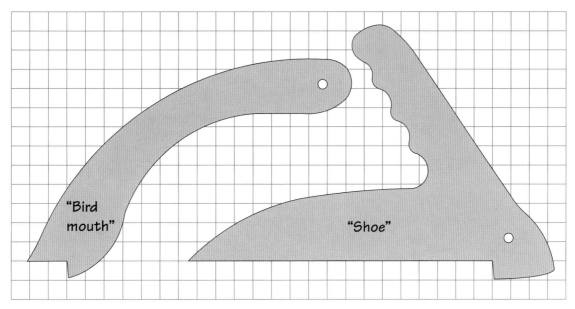

"Bird mouth"

"Shoe"

Enlarge 200% to create full-size patterns

Stanley Tool Cabinet

The man running the antiques booth was certain he'd found a sucker. I was fawning all over a well-preserved tool cabinet emblazoned with Stanley's "Sweetheart" logo — so called because it featured a heart with the initials "S.W." inside. As I examined the piece, the dealer dropped the price bit by bit.

Finally, I looked up at the dealer. He smiled because he smelled a sale — until I told him I'd rather build one and walked away. For the next couple weeks I tried to research the cabinet, but I couldn't find a photo or drawing of it in any of our old Stanley catalogs. The cabinet I examined looked similar to the old #862 from the early 1920s, but it wasn't quite right. So I gave up and built this one from memory and my notes. This cabinet is similar to the #862, but it's 1¾" deeper, has a small drawer at the bottom and is made from maple instead of a dark-stained oak. A great feature of this cabinet (and the #862) is the large handle on top of the cabinet. This makes it portable when you need to take your tools on a job — or when you quit your job. Cabinetmakers are an itinerant bunch.

Schedule of Materials • Stanley Tool Cabinet

No.	Ltr.	Item	Dimensions T W L	Material
2	A	Sides	3/4" x 8" x 22"	Maple
2	B	Top & bottom	3/4" x 8" x 14"	Maple
1	C	Divider	3/4" x 3 3/4" x 12 1/2"	Maple
1	D	Back	1/2" x 13 1/2" x 21 1/2"	Plywood
1	E	Front panel	1/2" x 13 1/4" x 21 1/4"	Plywood
1	F	Drawer front	3/4" x 4" x 12 1/2"	Maple
2	G	Sides	1/2" x 4" x 3 1/4"	Plywood
1	H	Back	1/2" x 3 1/2" x 12"	Plywood
1	I	Bottom	1/4" x 3" x 12"	Plywood

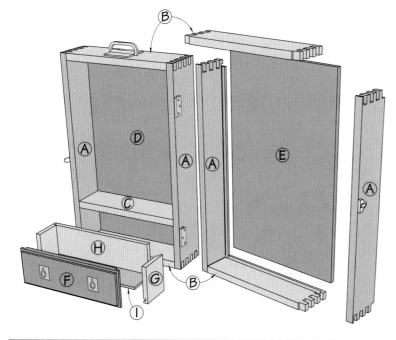

Construction

I built this cabinet and door as one box and then parted the front door off using my table saw. It's tricky to keep the blade from binding during this operation, but I'll show you a way to make this procedure safer. The case itself is assembled using rugged finger joints. The back panel rests in a rabbet. The front panel sits in a groove on all four sides, and the drawer divider is biscuited into place. Begin construction by cutting your parts to size according to the schedule of materials.

First, cut the 1/2" finger joints on the ends of the top, bottom and sides. I use a homemade jig for my table saw like the one shown in the photo. Now cut the 1/2"×1/2" stopped rabbet for the back panel on the back inside edge of the four sides. Then cut the groove to hold the front panel. The front panel rests in a 1/2"-wide by 3/8"-deep groove that's 1/4" in from the front edge of the sides. Now cut the biscuit slots for the drawer di-

HERE'S HOW TO CUT THE FINGER JOINTS • Put a dado stack in your table saw to make a 1/2"-wide cut. Raise your blade just a hair over 3/4". The jig is a piece of plywood screwed to the miter gauge. First attach the plywood to your gauge, then make a cut in the plywood using your dado stack. Now cut a small piece of plywood that's exactly 1/2" x 1/2" x 3/4". Glue and screw this block exactly 1/2" away from the cut on the plywood as shown in the photo. Cutting your finger joints is now simple.

vider, which is 4¾" up from the bottom edge of the sides. Make sure the divider is flush to the back panel when the case is assembled.

Get out your clamps and assemble the case without glue. The front panel should square up the case. Now assemble the case again, this time with glue.

Finally, it's time to part the front door off the case. As I mentioned before, this can be tricky. Get out a hot-melt glue gun and eight 6"-long blocks of wood. Glue two of these to the inside of each side of the box. These blocks will hold the box together, and the kerf open, as you cut the case on the table saw.

Now set your table saw's rip fence to 4¼" and raise the blade to just over ¾". Make sure the back part of the cabinet is running against the fence. First, cut along the top, then one side, then the bottom and the other side. Pry the blocks loose after the cut and remove the glue with a scraper.

Drawer Construction

The drawer is a simple thing that's great for holding hardware. Here's how I built it: the ½"-thick drawer sides rest in ½"×¼" rabbets on the ends of the drawer front. The back rests in ½"×¼" rabbets in the sides. And the ¼"-thick drawer bottom rests in a ¼"×¼" groove in the sides and front that's ¼" up from the bottom edge. I also cut a ¼"×¼" rabbet on the drawer front as a decorative detail.

Glue your drawer together, then nail the sides to the front and back. Nail the bottom in place to the back.

Now attach all the hardware. The drawer gets two finger pulls. Screw two cabinet hangers to the back so your cabinet can be hung on the wall. Don't forget the handle on the top. Also, put two screws at the bottom of the back piece to allow you to level it against the wall.

Finally, protect your cabinet with three coats of clear finish and nail the back in place. Hang it above your bench using wall anchors, but don't make those screws too tight. You never know when you might have to change jobs.

SPLITTING THE CABINET
Use hot-melt glue to attach 6"-long blocks (inset) that keep the saw kerf open when you cut the front off the cabinet. After that, ripping the cabinet is almost cake.

Supplies

Available at any hardware store:
2- Butt Hinges

Available from most woodworking catalogs: Magnetic Tool Strip

Available from Lee Valley Tools, (800) 871-8158, www.leevalley.com:
2- Flush Ring Pulls - $10.95 ea.
   Item # 00L02.01
1- Chest Handle - $11.75 pr.
   Item # 06W02.01
1- Draw Catch - $3.95 pr.
   Item # 00S70.01

Table Saw
Organizer

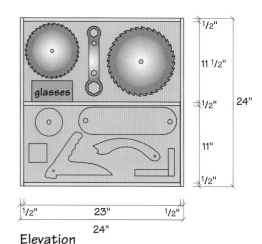

Plan

1/2" 2" 3" 1/2"

1/2" 23" 1/2"
24"

Construction

Start by cutting the parts out according to the schedule of materials. Nail the top and bottom to the edge of the back, and nail the shelf to the back in the location shown in the diagram. Nail the sides on and attach iron-on maple veneer tape to all the front edges. Glue and nail wood edging to the drop front. Install the hinges and mount the door to the main assembly. Attach the chains to the door and the main assembly. Use a magnetic catch to hold the door closed.

Interior Storage

Drill and glue the ½" dowels for the saw blades into the back. Put the case

on its back and place your odds and ends in their future resting places. Mark the nail and screw locations for hanging these objects and install them. Two special tips for hanging a tape measure and a square are as follows: For the tape, screw a piece of old belt leather to the back and the tape measure's clip should slide right in. For the square, cut a small rabbet in scrap that is the length of the square's blade. Screw the wood piece to the back and hang the square by the blade.

Final Touches

Attach the pull, then remove the hardware. Apply two coats of clear finish. Hang it, load it and get to work!

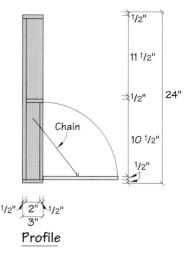

Elevation

1/2"
11 1/2"
1/2"
11"
1/2"
24"

1/2" 23" 1/2"
24"

glasses

Profile

1/2"
11 1/2"
1/2"
10 1/2"
1/2"
24"

Chain

1/2" 2" 1/2"
3"

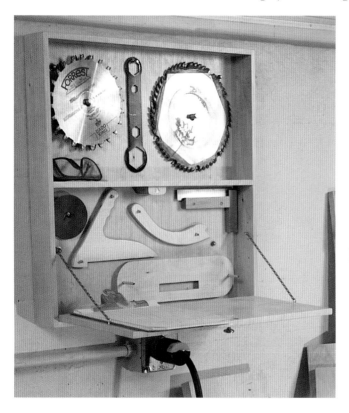

Schedule of Materials • Table Saw Organizer

No.	Ltr.	Item	Dimensions T W L	Material
1	A	Back	½" x 23" x 23"	Plywood
2	B	Top & bottom	½" x 3" x 23"	Plywood
1	C	Shelf	½" x 2½" x 23"	Plywood
1	D	Sides	½" x 3" x 24"	Plywood
1	E	Drop front	½" x 10¾" x 22¾"*	Plywood
1	F	Dowel rod	½" x 12"	Hardwood
1	F	Wood trim	⅛" x ⅝" x 72"	Maple

*Sized without trim

Lathe
Tool Cabinet

Schedule of Materials • Lathe Tool Cabinet

No.	Item	Dimensions T W L	Material
2	Top & bottom	$1/2$" × $10^{1/2}$" × $23^{1/2}$"	Birch Ply
1	Horiz. divider	$1/2$" × $9^{1/4}$" × $23^{1/2}$"	Birch Ply
2	Sides	$1/2$" × $10^{1/2}$" × $25^{1/2}$"	Birch Ply
1	Back	$1/2$" × $23^{1/2}$" × 25"	Birch Ply
2	Doors	$3/4$" × $11^{1/4}$" × $18^{3/4}$"	Birch Ply
1	Drawer front	$3/4$" × $4^{3/4}$" × $4^{3/4}$"	Birch Ply
1	Drawer front	$3/4$" × $4^{3/4}$" × $17^{1/4}$"	Birch Ply
4	Drawer sides	$1/2$" × $1^{1/2}$" × 12"	Birch Ply
1	Drawer back	$1/2$" × 5" × $17^{1/4}$"	Birch Ply
1	Drawer back	$1/2$" × 5" × $4^{3/4}$"	Birch Ply
1	Drawer bottom	$1/4$" × $4^{1/2}$" × $8^{1/4}$"	Birch Ply
1	Drawer bottom	$1/4$" × 17" × $8^{1/4}$"	Birch Ply
2	Tool dividers	$1/2$" × 2" × 23"	Birch Ply
1	Tool-rest back	$1/2$" × $19^{1/2}$" × 23"	Birch Ply
1	Tool-rest base	$1/2$" × $2^{1/2}$" × 23"	Birch Ply
1	Tool-rest lip	$1/2$" × $1^{3/4}$" × 23"	Birch Ply
2	French cleats	$3/4$" × $3^{3/4}$" × 23"	Birch Ply
	Cockbeading	$1/8$" × $1^{3/16}$" × 15"	Maple

Case Construction

Start by cutting the parts. Cut a $1/2$"×$1/4$"-deep groove in the top, bottom and sides for the back as shown in the diagram. Then cut a $1/2$"×$1/4$"-deep rabbet in the top and bottom edge of both sides. Next cut a $1/2$"×$1/4$"-deep dado in the sides for the horizontal divider, located as shown. Assemble the case, back and horizontal divider; then nail in the drawer divider. Apply birch veneer tape to the front edges of the case.

Tool Rest

Make the tool divider by drilling 1" holes in a piece of stock, then assemble the tool-rest parts and drawers according to the diagram. Screw the tool rest to the case.

Doors and Drawers

Miter and attach the cockbeading to the doors and drawer fronts. Make the drawers, then attach the drawer fronts to the drawers. Hang the doors using butt hinges with the hinge barrels in-line with the cockbeading. Attach the pulls and disassemble the cabinet. Apply three coats of clear finish and you're ready to hang it on the wall and store your tools.

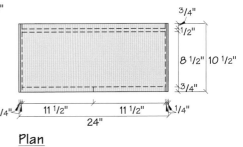

Elevation

Profile

Plan

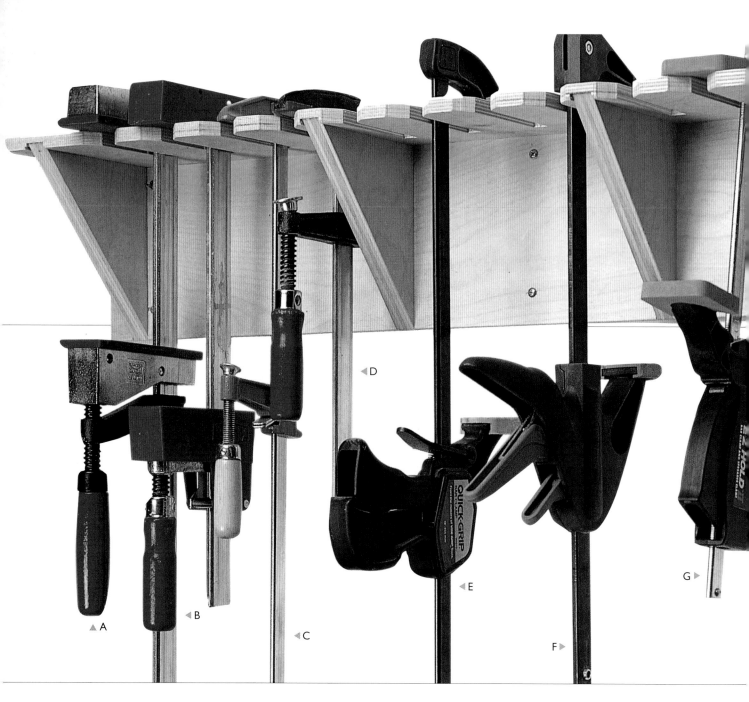

You may never have enough clamps, but those you do are always in need of a handy place to call home. You could simply nail a 2×4 to your wall, or build the complex rolling clamp rack in the next chapter. We were looking for a happy medium that would be versatile enough to handle a number of clamp designs, and we came up with this simple six-piece wall-mounted clamp rack.

Construction is simple. We chose ½" birch plywood for the top and back — it offers enough support and strength without looking clunky. The triangular braces are made from ¾" plywood

rather than ½" — primarily to make it easier to get screws into the brace.

Start by cutting a piece of ½" plywood to 12⅛"×36", then cut the four dadoes as shown in the diagram. If you change the length of the clamp rack, make sure there are no more than four clamp slots between braces to ensure adequate support. I used a dado stack in my table saw to make the dadoes. When complete, remove the dado stack, reset the saw's rip fence for 6" and rip the piece in half, forming the top and back pieces.

Next, mark the top piece for the slots, again as shown on the diagram.

The ½"×4" slot holds the majority of clamps on the market today. Your clamp rack might perform better with a different-size slot, so check your clamps and adjust the dimensions if necessary.

The clipped corners at the entrance to the slots guide the clamp bar into the slot without banging up the slot. Unless you have a band saw with a very deep throat you will not be able to cut all the slots on your band saw. You may choose to use a jigsaw on all the slots, or use your band saw on some and finish the rest with a jigsaw.

With the slots cut, move on to the braces. The finished brace is a triangle

Wall-Mounted
Clamp Rack

◄ H

KNOW YOUR CLAMPS

Parallel Clamps

Parallel clamps are designed to maintain the same spacing between the jaws along the entire depth of the jaw. Beneficial for panel and box work, as well as general use, these clamps are heavy duty—and so are the prices.

  A - Gross Stabil Parallel

  B - Bessey K-Body

F-Style Bar Clamps

These steel bar clamps have been the industry standard for years in a number of different duty ratings. With the introduction of parallel clamps, bar clamps have become more popular as a light- or medium-weight clamp.

  C - Jorgensen Light Duty

  D - Bessey Tradesman

One-Handed Clamps

Fast-adjust, or one-handed, clamps are relatively new in the market, but have gained a strong following. Rated from light-duty to heavy-duty, they offer rapid one-handed tightening and release for complicated glue-ups or for quick clamping during assembly. Some also convert to spreader clamps.

  E - Original Quick-Grip

  F - Wolfcraft

  G - Jorgensen E-Z Hold II

  H - Bessey Power Grip

measuring $5^{11}/_{16}"\times6^{3}/_{16}"$ on the two legs. You can save material by interlocking the brackets. Cut the four braces and sand the leading edge to avoid sharp edges.

Mark the top and back pieces for clearance holes used to screw the braces in place. Then drill the $^{3}/_{16}"$ clearance holes and countersink for a flathead screw. I nailed the top onto the back to hold the rack's "corner" flush while drilling a pilot hole into the braces. Now glue and screw the entire rack together.

Sand all the sharp edges, then go find some studs to hang your rack.

Details

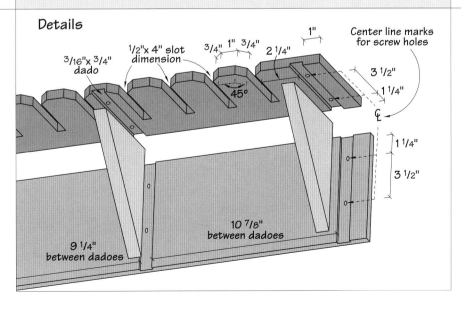

$^{3}/_{16}"$ x $^{3}/_{4}"$ dado

$^{1}/_{2}"$ x 4" slot dimension

$^{3}/_{4}"$ 1" $^{3}/_{4}"$

2 $^{1}/_{4}"$

1"

45°

Center line marks for screw holes

3 $^{1}/_{2}"$

1 $^{1}/_{4}"$

C̶L

1 $^{1}/_{4}"$

3 $^{1}/_{2}"$

10 $^{7}/_{8}"$ between dadoes

9 $^{1}/_{4}"$ between dadoes

Rolling
Clamp Rack

When you've got so many clamps that it's a problem getting them to where the work is being done, build this rolling clamp rack! It holds about 50 clamps, takes up a little more than four square feet of floor space and can honestly be built in an afternoon. The construction of the frame is simple, but the "hanging" part of the rack depends a great deal on the type and variety of clamps you own.

Construction

Cut the ends of the four uprights and the two base support pieces at a 10-degree angle as shown. Assemble the two side frames by screwing two cross supports between the pairs of uprights, holding the top inside edge of the support flush to the inside of the upright, and flush to the top or bottom 10-degree angles. Attach the two frames together to form the "A" by screwing the base supports and the top supports to the sides of the frames, holding them

flush to the bottom and top of the frames. Now attach the casters to the outside ends of the two lower cross supports. Consider your clamps and how they can best be stored on the two slanted sides of the rack, and notch the clamp supports accordingly. Then screw the supports between the uprights. I used an extra cross support screwed to the top of the rack for storing hand screws and spring clamps. I also added two notched strips to the sides for storing smaller clamps.

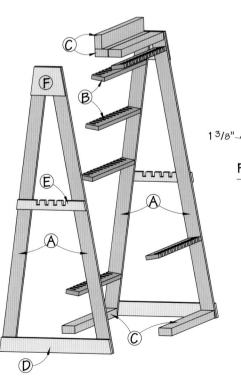

Each $^3/4$" x $1 ^1/2$"notch is equally spaced from the given inset. Your clamps may require different notch sizes.

$1 ^3/8$"

$1 ^1/2$"

$1 ^3/8$"

$1 ^1/4$" $3/4$"

Plan of clamp holder "B"

Schedule of Materials • Rolling Clamp Rack

No.	Ltr.	Item	Dimensions T W L	Material
4	A	Uprights	$^3/4$" x 3" x $61^1/2$"	Poplar
6	B	Clamp holders	$^7/8$" x 3" x $25^1/2$"	Poplar
5	C	Cross supports	$1^5/8$" x 3" x $25^1/2$"	Poplar
2	D	Base supports	$^7/8$" x 3" x 26"	Poplar
2	E	Side clamp holders	$^7/8$" x 2" x 16"	Poplar
2	F	Top supports	$^1/2$" x 8" x 6"	Plywood

Stacking Storage Boxes

In any workshop, efficient storage is very important, especially if your workshop space is at a premium. These storage boxes can snuggle up against a wall in an otherwise useless corner of your workshop. While they are a good, solid box that you can tote from one place to another — unlike most storage boxes — once these are stacked you still have access to the contents of the lower boxes.

Assemble the Ends

Assemble the ends by placing a 5½"-wide end piece in the middle of two 3½" end pieces. Separate them slightly by placing a business card between each piece at the top and bottom. Offset the middle piece ¾" higher than the two side pieces, using a scrap piece of wood as a guide. This "notch" is used to lock the storage boxes together when they are stacked. Screw two battens to the ends so they are flush to the front and back edges and even with the top and bottom of the 3½"-wide pieces.

Build the Backs ...

For the backs, screw a bottom ledger onto one 5½"-wide side piece so that it is centered and flush with the bottom edge. Then, lay out first a 1½"-wide piece and another 5½"-wide piece, and screw the three together using two battens. The battens are held ¼" down from the top and 2" in from the ends.

... And the Doors

To make the doors, use two 5½"-wide pieces and attach the battens ¼" from the top and 2" from the ends. Screw the bottom ledger to the 1½"-wide front piece, flush to the top and bottom and centered end to end. Place the two front parts faceup and attach the hinges.

Put It All Together

Glue and screw the back to the outside of the ends, then glue and screw the lower front to the ends. Finally screw the bottom in place, making sure it rests on the ledgers on all sides. The door is held closed by eye hooks attached at the ends, and handles are screwed to both ends of the box. You can leave the box natural if desired, or give it two light coats of polyurethane varnish for extra protection.

by Michel Theriault
Michel Theriault, a woodworker in Ottawa, Canada, has written over 100 magazine and newspaper articles based on his work.

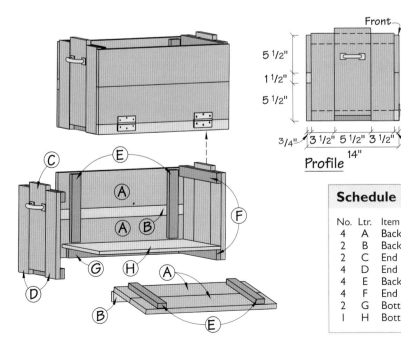

Front
¾"
¼"
5 ½"
5 ½"
1 ½"
5 ½"
13 ½"
5 ½"
¾"
¾" 3 ½" 5 ½" 3 ½" ¾"
Profile 14"

Schedule of Materials • Stacking Storage Boxes

No.	Ltr.	Item	Dimensions T W L	Material
4	A	Back & door pieces	¾" x 5½" x 22"	Pine
2	B	Back & front pieces	¾" x 1½" x 22"	Pine
2	C	End pieces	¾" x 5½" x 12¾"	Pine
4	D	End pieces	¾" x 3½" x 12¾"	Pine
4	E	Back & door battens	¾" x 1½" x 10"	Pine
4	F	End battens	¾" x 1½" x 12½"	Pine
2	G	Bottom ledgers	¾" x 1½" x 19"	Pine
1	H	Bottom	½" x 12½" x 20½"	Plywood

Hand
Screws

When purchasing hand screws, you can save more than 50 percent by making the wooden part of the clamp yourself from shop scraps. Kits for clamps in a variety of sizes are available at many hardware stores and through mail order.

The clamp I built has jaws that open 6". Different-size clamps will have different-size wooden blocks, commonly called "chops." But the way you build them is the same.

Size the Wood
Cut the chops to the size indicated by your hardware kit from a suitable hardwood, such as maple, walnut or oak. Make sure the long sides are flat and square to each other.

Making the Holes
Mark the locations for the holes on all four sides of each chop. Depending on the kit and the size of clamp you're making, you might have to purchase an odd-sized bit for the holes. (My kit called for a bit that was $^{37}/_{64}$". I used a bit that was $^1/_{64}$" smaller, $^9/_{16}$", and a little easier to find.) First bore the holes in the sides of each chop that hold the metal nuts. Then drill the holes for the

threaded spindles in the top and bottom. These holes are angled and intersect with the holes drilled in the sides. Some instruction books recommend you drill these angled holes while rocking the chop back and forth against a fence on your drill press to clean out the waste. Instead, angle the drill press table, then clamp the chop to the table. Chain-drill several holes of ascending depths; clean out the hole with a chisel. Clean up your sloped holes with a rat-tail file.

Clean and Trim
Cut the angled top on each chop with a band saw. Bevel all the outside edges of the chops using a sander or a router. Don't bevel the inside edges that make up the clamp's jaws. Apply an oil finish on the chops; allow to dry.

Assemble
Assemble the hand screws by inserting the end nuts into the holes in each chop and then threading the two spindles through those nuts. Attach the handles by tapping each one onto the end of a spindle. Drill a hole through the ferrule, handle and spindle. Insert the supplied rivet into the hole and peen it for a secure hold.

Supplies

From Rockler,
(800) 279-4441:
6" Jaw Opening - $12.95
Item #42523
8½" Jaw Opening - $14.95
Item #42531

From Leichtung,
(800) 321-6840:
6" Jaw Opening - $7.99
Item #71605
8½" Jaw Opening - $8.99
Item #71613

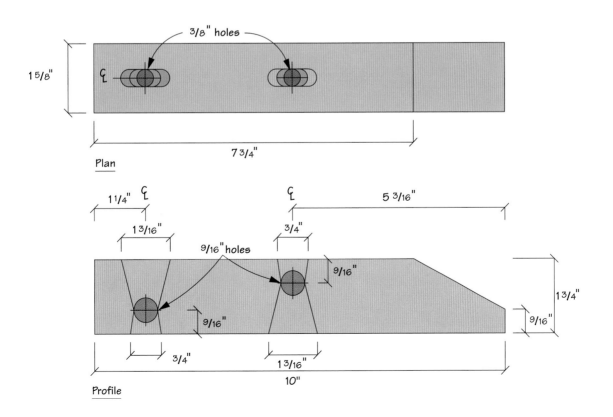

Plan

3/8" holes

1 5/8"

7 3/4"

Profile

1 1/4"

5 3/16"

1 3/16"

3/4"

9/16" holes

9/16"

9/16"

1 3/4"

9/16"

3/4"

1 3/16"

10"

Schedule of Materials • Sharpening Kit

No.	Item	Dimensions T W L	Material
2	Lid and bottom	$\frac{1}{2}$" x $9\frac{1}{8}$" x 14"	Plywood
2	Ends	$\frac{1}{2}$" x $2\frac{3}{8}$" x $10\frac{1}{8}$"	Maple
2	Sides	$\frac{1}{2}$" x $2\frac{3}{8}$" x 15"	Maple
2	Clamp blocks	$\frac{3}{4}$" x 1" x 6"	Maple

Approximately 4' of $\frac{3}{8}$" x $\frac{3}{4}$" divider strips and a piece of $\frac{1}{4}$" plywood in the top big enough to retain the stones.

Sharpening Kit

I used to keep my sharpening stones wrapped in grimy old towels that I threw into a beat-up army duffel bag. This was a risky way to carry around $75 worth of stones — one false move could break these brittle beauties.

So I designed this nifty briefcase to hold my stones, honing oil and even a homemade clamp that secures the stones while I'm using them. The briefcase handle (which I bought at a hardware store for a few bucks) slides easily into the tail vise on my bench to hold the case fast while I'm at work. Thanks to these little innovations, sharpening is easier.

Cut and Assemble

Cut the pieces of the outside shell to size according to the schedule of materials. Miter the corners of the four sides and biscuit the plywood lid and bottom into the four sides. Glue, clamp and allow to dry. I used polyurethane glue, which might be overkill, but I figured with all the honing oil leaching into the box, I'd rather be safe than sorry.

Split the Box

Clean up the outside edges of the box and cut the box lengthwise on your table saw to make a top and bottom. I set my rip fence for $1\frac{1}{4}$" for this cut, which makes the top of the box slightly smaller than the base and lets my thickest stone protrude $\frac{1}{4}$" above the edge of the bottom so I can grab it easily. Lay out and mount the hinges.

Fit-Out the Interior

Build the clamp from scrap hardwood. Cut a $\frac{1}{4}$"×$\frac{1}{4}$" rabbet on one edge of each of the clamp pieces. This rabbet will hold the stones in place. Drill holes in the clamp pieces and the side of the box for the 4"-long $\frac{1}{4}$" bolts. I put compression springs on the bolts between the clamps, and washers and wing nuts on the outside. The clamp works great. Now comes the custom part. Measure your stones and build compartments for them with $\frac{3}{8}$"×$\frac{3}{8}$" strips of hardwood. I used Super Glue to affix the wood. Then cut and glue strips of plywood into the bottom of each compartment to get all the stones to sit at the same level. I glued a piece of $\frac{1}{4}$" plywood to the inside of the lid to keep the stones from rattling.

Finishing Touches

Remove the clamp hardware and close the box. Put a $\frac{1}{4}$" roundover on all the outside edges, including the corners. Mount the briefcase handle and catches on the front of the box. Then put a couple coats of an oil finish on the box, and you're ready to go.

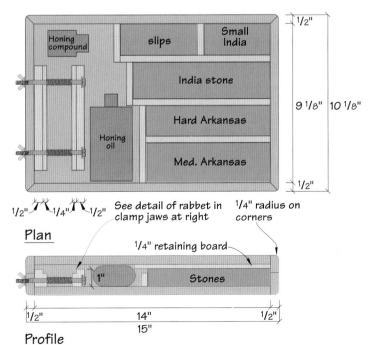

Plan

Profile

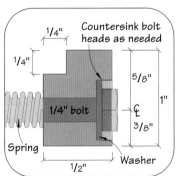

Full-size detail of Clamp Block

Tilting Router Stand

A tilting router stand makes the router easily accessible and lets you secure the router to the table. The table swings up like the lid of a chest, exposing the router and bringing it up to a comfortable working height. You can change bits and make adjustments standing upright, just like the Deity intended.

Of course, to get this amazing convenience, you have to build a complex mechanism and a special table, right? Nope. Most parts are rectangular boards, butted together and secured with screws or bolts. The design is easily adaptable to support whatever table-top you're using right now; just change the width and depth of the stand to fit, or use the sizes on the diagrams.

Begin with the frame under the table. It should be about 6" smaller side-to-side and 4" smaller front-to-back than your router table. If the table has slots to mount the fence, make sure that the frame members won't cover these or interfere with the fence movement. Also give some thought to how

you will attach the table to the frame. I used two long cleats, one on each side. Brackets, table clips and pockets screws work equally well.

The legs should hold the table at countertop level — roughly 36". My router table is part of a "work island" — the table saw, workbench and router table are all at the same level. So I cut the legs on my table a fraction of an inch longer than the drawings show.

by Nick Engler

Nick is a contributing editor to *Popular Woodworking*. He's written 52 books on woodworking, and has invented more jigs and fixtures than he cares to count.

ROUTER CRANK

If you use a plunge router with your router table, this little gizmo takes all the frustration out of setting the depth of cut. Just thread it onto the post, then crank the router up and down as needed.

There's an accessory on the market very much like this, I know. But it has a simple knob at the top and takes a lot of wrist action to raise or lower the router. You'll find the crank action much faster and more comfortable. When used with the tilting router stand, the two fixtures create a truly user-friendly stationary routing system.

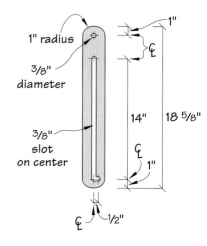

1" radius
3/8" diameter
3/8" slot on center
1"
14"
18 5/8"
1"
1/2"

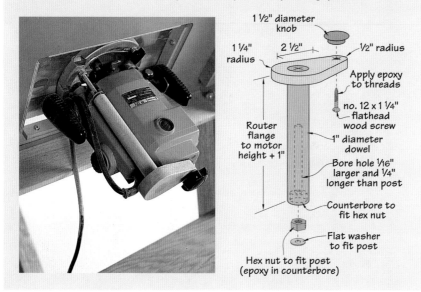

1 1/2" diameter knob
1 1/4" radius
2 1/2"
1/2" radius
Apply epoxy to threads
no. 12 x 1 1/4" flathead wood screw
Router flange to motor height + 1"
1" diameter dowel
Bore hole 1/16" larger and 1/4" longer than post
Counterbore to fit hex nut
Flat washer to fit post
Hex nut to fit post (epoxy in counterbore)

long slot with a little "hiccup" at one end. I made the hiccup first, drilling a few overlapping holes to create a short slot. I routed a long slot perpendicular to the short one, then cleaned up the edges of the short slot with a file. When mounting the support arm to the stand, the short portion of the slot faces front.

To help organize all my router bits and collars, I mounted two sliding shelves to the fixed shelf inside the storage box. You needn't purchase expensive hardware to get the sliding action. Make narrow hardwood rails to guide the shelves, then cut matching grooves in the sliding shelves and fixed rails. Glue splines in the grooves in the rails, then glue the rails to a fixed shelf. Fit the sliding shelves to the splined

A plywood box is screwed to the legs below the table to brace the legs and provide storage for router accessories. There must be adequate room between the top of the box and the bottom of the router table to fit the router when

the collet is fully retracted into the router base. I mounted simple plywood doors on the front legs to enclose the box and keep some of the sawdust out.

The most complex part in the table is the support arm. It has an L-slot — a

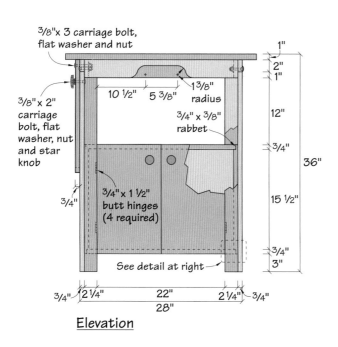

3/8" x 3 carriage bolt, flat washer and nut
1"
2"
1"
10 1/2"   5 3/8"
1 3/8" radius
3/8" x 2" carriage bolt, flat washer, nut and star knob
3/4" x 3/8" rabbet
12"
3/4"
36"
3/4"
3/4" x 1 1/2" butt hinges (4 required)
15 1/2"
See detail at right
3/4"
3"
3/4" 2 1/4"   22"   2 1/4" 3/4"
28"

Elevation

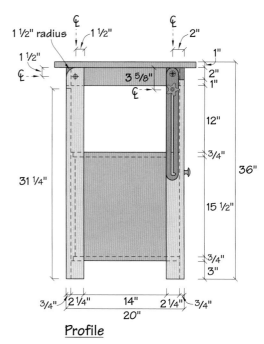

1 1/2" radius   1 1/2"   2"
1 1/2"
1"
3 5/8"
2"
1"
12"
31 1/4"
3/4"
36"
15 1/2"
3/4"
3"
3/4" 2 1/4"   14"   2 1/4" 3/4"
20"

Profile

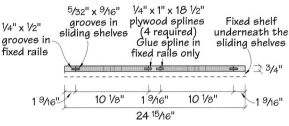

1/4" x 1/2" grooves in fixed rails

5/32" x 9/16" grooves in sliding shelves

1/4" x 1" x 18 1/2" plywood splines (4 required) Glue spline in fixed rails only

Fixed shelf underneath the sliding shelves

3/4"

1 9/16" 10 1/8" 1 9/16" 10 1/8" 1 9/16"

24 15/16"

Elevation of sliding shelves

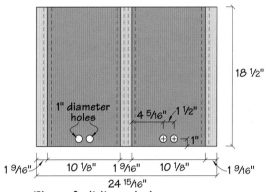

18 1/2"

1" diameter holes

4 5/16" 1 1/2"

1"

1 9/16" 10 1/8" 1 9/16" 10 1/8" 1 9/16"

24 15/16"

Plan of sliding shelves

The sliding shelves shown in the photo are removable so you can take your bits where they are needed.

guides, enlarging the grooves in the edges and sanding a little stock from the bottom faces so the shelves slide easily. Wax the grooves in the shelves to help them move smoothly. I drilled holes and mounted dowels in the sliding trays to help organize the bits and accessories and keep them in place. The shelves slide all the way out of the storage box so you can use them as a caddy or tray to carry the bits.

To raise the top of the router table, lift it all the way up and push down near the bottom of the support arm to slip the locking bolt into the short portion of the L-slot. Tighten the knob to make sure the top doesn't slam down unexpectedly.

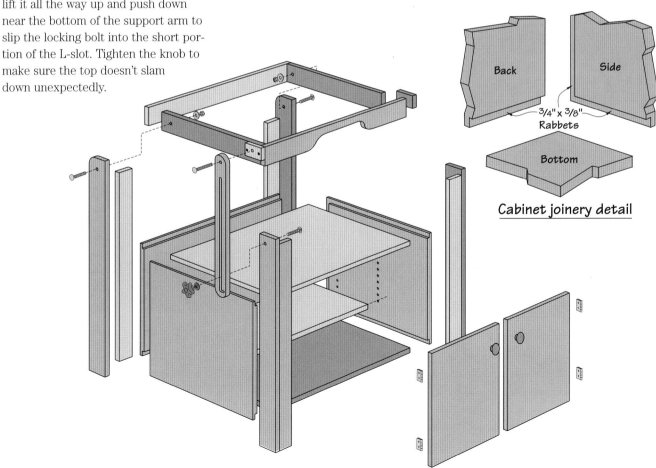

Back Side

3/4" x 3/8" Rabbets

Bottom

Cabinet joinery detail

Table Saw
Tenon Jig

The first tenoning jig I built years ago. It's seen a lot of use on my table saw and my router. When I went to build a new jig, I realized that this one served me so well that I didn't need to add any more features to make it more useful.

Several years ago my brother-in-law was thinking about buying a commercial tenoning jig because he was having trouble keeping his work flat against his table saw's small fence while cutting tenon cheeks.

"Don't do that," I told him. "I'll show you how to build a jig from a few pieces of scrap that will do the job just fine." So I built the jig in the photo above and have used it just about every day in my shop to cut tenons on my table saw and sliding dovetails on my router table. The high side and back keep my tenons in position as I cut the cheeks. It's difficult to mess up a tenon with this jig.

When I decided to retire the old jig and build a new one, I thought about adding some fancy features. Then I realized that simple is best, and I stuck

with my original design. This jig is built to be used with a commercial Biesemeyer fence. If you don't have a Biesemeyer, you'll have to change the dimensions of the top and side runners, but that's simple to do.

Simplicity Itself

Basically, this jig is two pieces of plywood in an L shape that have a couple pieces of wood screwed to them to allow them to ride the table saw's fence. After settling on the dimensions that are right for your fence, cut all your pieces to size. First clamp the side piece and top runner in position on your fence. Mark where the two pieces intersect, and screw and glue the two

Here's the side piece held in place against the top runner. You want the top runner to be snug against the top of your fence.

by Glen Huey
Glen Huey, of Middletown, Ohio, is a contributing editor to *Popular Woodworking*.

The triangular braces keep the side and top runner square and sturdy for years to come.

Take your time fitting the corner brace between the side and back pieces. You want it to hold these pieces at exactly 90 degrees.

Mortise-and-tenon joints are the staple of my custom woodworking business. I use this jig on every piece of furniture I build. The jig's simplicity and sturdiness have made it one of the workhorses in my shop.

Schedule of Materials • Table Saw Tenon Jig

No.	Ltr.	Item	Dimensions T W L	Material
1	A	Back	$3/4$" x 10" x $15\frac{1}{4}$"	Plywood
1	B	Side	$3/4$" x 10" x 16"	Plywood
1	C	Top runner	$3/4$" x $4\frac{3}{4}$" x 16"	Plywood
1	D	Side runner	$3/4$" x $2\frac{1}{2}$" x 16"	Plywood
2	E	Triangular braces	$3/8$" x 3" x $7\frac{1}{2}$"	Plywood
1	F	Corner brace	$7/8$" x 1" x 21"	Hardwood*

* Piece is long; cut to fit.

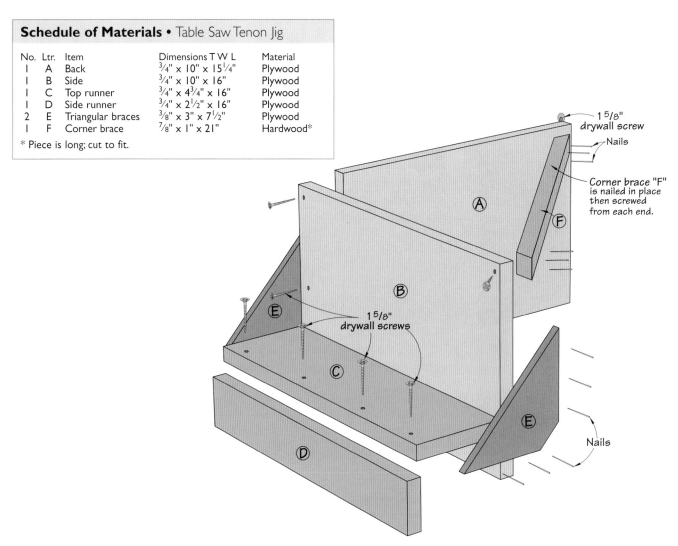

$1\frac{5}{8}$" drywall screw

Nails

Corner brace "F" is nailed in place then screwed from each end.

Ⓐ

Ⓕ

Ⓑ

Ⓔ

$1\frac{5}{8}$" drywall screws

Ⓒ

Ⓔ

Nails

Ⓓ

Furniture wax works great to keep the runners moving smoothly over your fence. Be sure to reapply wax when the jig starts to get a little stiff after use.

After making the cheek cuts (shown in the opening photo of this chapter), reset the saw to define the tenon's edge cheeks.

The curly maple board attached to my miter gauge minimizes tear-out when I make the shoulder cuts for my tenons.

pieces together. Be sure to countersink the screw heads in the side piece. Position the side runner in place under the top runner. You want it to be tight against the fence — but not too tight. Screw it into place.

Now glue and screw the large back piece to the side piece. You want the angle to be 90 degrees between the two pieces, so check your work. Later you'll add a corner brace that will keep this angle fixed at 90 degrees. Attach the two triangular braces to the side and runners. Attach the braces with nails and glue.

Now miter the corner brace to fit. Put an engineer's square between the back and side and adjust the brace until it holds these pieces at exactly 90 degrees. Now nail the brace in place.

Setup and Use

Before you go cutting tenons, wax the areas of the runners that come in contact with your fence. If your jig won't slide, unscrew the side runner and take a light jointer pass on it. When the jig slides smoothly, add some glue to the joint between the side and top runner to make it permanent.

Cutting tenons is now simple. First use your miter gauge and fence to define your shoulders. Then put your jig up on the saw and make your cheek cuts.

SANDING TIPS

SMALL–PIECE SANDING MADE E-Z • Sanding small parts can be tough without this trick in your workshop magic bag. All you need is a clipboard, a couple of spring clips (any office supply store) and a sheet of sandpaper. Slide the sandpaper into the clipboard, using the spring clips to hold the edges. Then sand away on those teeny-tiny parts without any of the usual fuss and bother.

CHEAP FLAP SANDER • Sanding the inside of a hole can be a major hassle, especially if the hole is too small for any of your drum sanders. The solution is to take a short piece of dowel and cut a deep notch in one end — carefully, of course. Cut a piece of sandpaper so it's a few inches long and as wide as the slot you just cut in the dowel. Put one end of the sandpaper strip into the notched dowel, grit-side facing out, and then chuck the dowel into a drill. Wrap the sandpaper strip loosely around the dowel in a clockwise direction. Your flap sander is ready for use. If the strip starts to work loose, use a hot-melt glue gun to put a dab of adhesive to hold it in place.

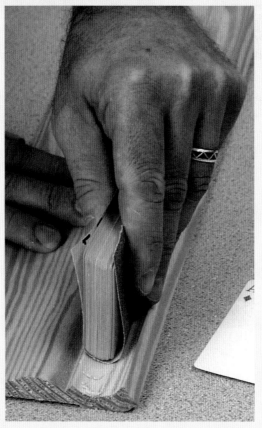

ACES HIGH • Sanding contours is never much fun. So break out a deck of cards, but not for the reason you may think. Wrap the card deck (or a portion of it that matches the area to be sanded) in your sandpaper, adjusting the deck so it matches the shape of the piece to be sanded. What that deck of cards has become is a contour sander that can be adjusted to fit even the most complex shapes. Plus you can always take a break from your sanding chores and indulge in some workshop solitaire.

HOSE IT DOWN • **A piece of old garden hose makes a flexible and inexpensive sanding tool when dealing with curves, contours and rounded sections. Slit one side of the hose open and trim the sandpaper to fit. It should wrap around the outside of the hose with the ends going into the slit. If you're going to use this trick, be sure the old hose you use is still flexible. Good-quality rubber is the best. No old hose? Hardware stores usually have short sections available, and they're cheap.**

SANDPAPER TIPS

Some quick tips for getting your money's worth from sandpaper:

• Keep it flat. The paper will absorb humidity and curl if left out in the open. Keep it in the package until use, or build a simple lidded storage tray that puts some weight on the sandpaper, keeping it squished flat.

• You can make sandpaper that will be used on a power sander stronger by applying a layer of duct tape to the back of the sandpaper. The tape will make the paper less likely to tear and also seems to help it cut a bit better.

• Clean the buildup from belt sanders with a soft rubber belt cleaner. You can buy these from woodworking stores cheaply, but the back of your closet may hold some old rubber-soled gym shoes that will perform the same function.

4–SQUARE SANDPAPER CUTTER • **Mount an old hacksaw blade under a wooden stick stiffener on either side of a scrap piece of plywood. Put a stop in the middle. On one side, tear a full-size sheet of sandpaper in half. Put that cut half on the other side and tear it in half. Voilà! You've got a quarter-size sheet of sandpaper perfect for your pad sander or sanding block.**

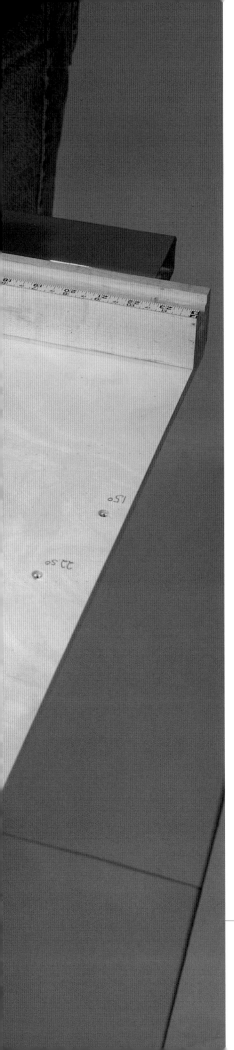

Table Saw
Miter Sled

I've tried out dozens of table saws over the years, and the one thing I've come to expect on all makes and models is the miter gauge that barely serves its purpose. Catalogs have come to the rescue with many excellent aftermarket miter-gauge replacements — but at what a price! I figured that I'm reasonably intelligent, so I should be able to make my own replacement for a lot less. Voilà! ... for less than $35 in hardware and a modest amount of wood, I'm now set. You can do it, too — just follow these steps.

Split Rail Fencing

I took the improved miter-gauge concept a step further and turned it into a miter sled. This gives me the opportunity to add a stop block with measuring tape, as well as a hold-down attachment. The sled itself is simply a piece of ½" Baltic birch plywood attached to the guide bar from my old miter gauge. The part that makes this table saw jig versatile happens at the fence.

Both the permanent fence and the miter fence are made the same way on the table saw. Start with four halves and mark the inside face and top surface. Next, set up the saw as shown in the photos and make mirror-image grooves the length of the fence parts.

To allow for some adjustability on the fixed fence, use a chisel to cut matching notches on both fence halves as shown in the diagrams. When glued together, the notches will allow a screw head to slide ½" to allow you to square up your fence to the saw blade.

When done making those cuts, check the slots' fit against the hardware, then glue the halves together using the top surface as the reference point, rather than the bottom. When the glue has cured, run the bottom edge of each fence over the jointer to make a square and even bottom surface. Then reset the jointer fence to a 45-degree angle and take a pass (or two) off the inside bottom edge of each fence to make a dust slot. This slot keeps any chips or dirt from holding your work away from the fence.

Mending Fences

The next step is to prepare the fences for attachment to the sled. This is where the fences become different. The fixed fence is attached with machine screws slipped through clearance holes in the fence and fastened to T-nuts recessed into the underside of the sled. Location of the clearance holes isn't critical, but the fence should be clamped in place (flush to the right edge of the sled) before drilling the holes. Start by cutting the fences to length.

The hole necessary for the barrel of the T-nut is larger in diameter than the clearance hole for the screw, so you

You don't have to spend $200 to make dead-on crosscuts and miters; we built this sled for $35 in hardware.

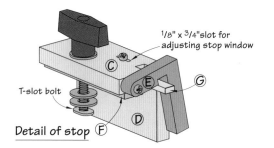

1/8" x 3/4" slot for
adjusting stop window

T-slot bolt

Detail of stop Ⓕ

Schedule of Materials • Table Saw Miter Sled

No.	Ltr.	Item	Dimensions T W L	Material
1	A	Sled	1/2" x 20" x 24"	Plywood
4	B	Fence halves	3/4" x 2" x 24"	Maple
1	C	Stop top	1/2" x 2 1/8" x 4"	Plywood
1	D	Stop face	1/2" x 1 7/8" x 4"	Plywood
1	E	Stop arm	1/2" x 2 1/4" x 2 1/4"	Plywood
2	F	Stop guides	3/16" x 3/4" x 4"	Maple
1	G	Stop window	3/16" x 3/8" x 4 7/8"	Plexiglas
1	H	Hold-down top	3/4" x 1 9/16" x 4"	Maple
1	I	Hold-down face	1/2" x 5 1/4" x 3 1/2"	Plywood

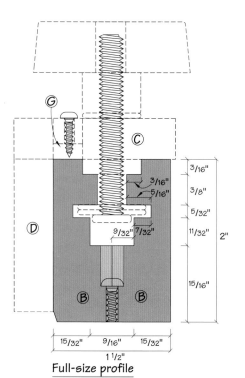

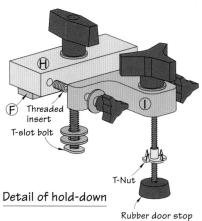

Threaded
insert

T-slot bolt

Detail of hold-down

T-Nut

Rubber door stop

3/16"
3/16"
3/8"
5/32"
11/32"
15/16"
2"

3/16"
5/16"
9/32" 7/32"

15/32" 9/16" 15/32"
1 1/2"

Full-size profile

Supplies

2- 1/4"-20, 1 1/4" stemmed knobs
6- 1/4" washers
2- 1/4"-20 x 1" knobs
2- no. 6 x 3/8" roundheaded screws
1- no. 6 x 1" roundheaded screw

**Available from Rockler,
(800) 279-4441, www.rockler.com:**
2- 5/16"-18 x 3 1/2" T-slot bolts
2- 5/16"-18 knobs
1- 5/16"-18 x 1 1/2" furniture glide
7- 1/4"-20 T-nuts
1- 3/8"-16 T-nut
2- 1/4"-20 threaded inserts

**Available from Woodhaven,
(800) 344-6657,
www.woodhaven.com:**
1- 24" right-to-left-reading tape

Make miter cuts with this sure-grip hold-down...

... or use the attachable featherboard for repeat cuts.

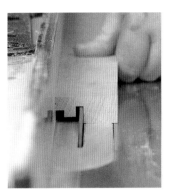
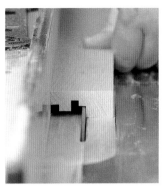

1 **IN THE GROOVE** • The first cut is made with the bottom of the piece against the table saw's fence, then the piece is turned around and the cut is finished to size. The next three cuts follow the same routine, changing the depth of cut and distance from the table saw fence for each.

2 **T–NUTS FOR ME** • Threaded inserts could be used to attach the fences to the sled, but they always seem to go in crooked. T-nuts are cheaper, easier to install and provide positive pull from the underside flange. One end of each fence and the recessed T-nuts are shown in the photo above. The last step on the fixed fence is to attach the right-to-left-reading adhesive measuring tape.

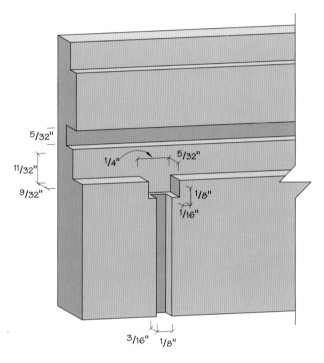

FENCE NOTCH CUTS • Chisel or band saw a ³/₁₆" x ¹/₈" dado a few inches in from the left end on each half of the fence. Then chisel a ⁹/₃₂" x ¹/₄" x ¹/₈" notch at the top of each dado to allow room for the screw head to recess and slide.

can drill a clearance hole straight through the fence and through the sled. The fixed screw hole at the right of the fence should then be counterbored to allow the screw's head to drop below the groove. The machine screw's head should be no larger than ³/₈" to clear the fence grooves.

The adjustable screw (on the left of the fence) has already been notched in the previous step, so all that's left is to drill the T-nut holes to the proper diameter and recess the holes ¹/₈" from the underside using a Forstner bit.

The miter fence is a little easier. Angle-cut the ends of the fence to form a tongue on each end and then round them. The ¹/₄" clearance holes are drilled in the center and ³/₄" in from the ends. The T-nuts are then inserted as before with locations on the sled for 15-, 22.5-, 30- and 45-degree stops.

Adjustable Stop

The stop attachment is designed to be used on either the fixed or mitering fence. Shown in the diagram, the stop is simply four pieces of wood and a clear plastic insert. The stop's top is first grooved and notched for the Plexiglas window, then two slots are formed by connecting drilled holes to allow the Plexiglas to be adjusted on the measuring tape as necessary.

Glue the faceplate to the underside of the top and glue a guide to the underside of the top to fit into the groove in the fences. Some fine adjustment may be necessary to allow the stop attachment to move freely. Use the full-size plan of the stop arm to cut and shape the arm. Then lightly clamp the arm in place, drill a clearance hole and screw the arm to the stop. With the arm in place, use a scratch awl to cut a groove in the Plexiglas, then use a dark putty stick to fill in the groove, wiping away the excess.

Hold-down

Sometimes a stop block isn't what you want. What you need is a hold-down device. To provide the most versatility, I opted for a convertible hold-down attachment. Using a top assembly similar to the stop attachment, I mounted two threaded inserts into the facing edge of the top and made two different hold-down attachments for different applications. The featherboard adjusts up and down to hold the work in place for repeat passes, such as dadoes, while allowing enough play to tap the piece over for the next pass. A rubber door stop on a piece of threaded rod with a handle locks the piece in place and keeps it there. Again, the handy T-nut comes into play.

I'm fairly certain some of our readers will take the ideas presented here and make them even better. If you do, let me know. And even if you don't make any changes, I guarantee you'll find this sled more useful than your "factory" miter slot gauge.

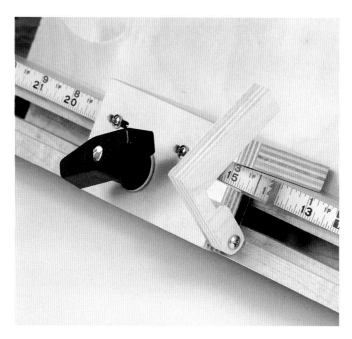

3 TWO-STAGE STOP • A feature we enjoy on this stop is the swing-up stop arm. This allows you to square cut one end of your piece (arm up), then swing the arm down and make the final length cut. No re-setting necessary. The hash mark on the window is set to the final cut size.

4 TWO-IN-ONE HOLD-DOWN • By using optional add-ons for the hold-down attachment, this hold-down serves two functions. You might think of a few more add-ons to make the miter sled even more versatile. The fingerboard is also shown.

Schedule of Materials • Sandpaper Press			
No.	Item	Dimensions T W L	Material
1	Bottom	3/4" x 9 1/8" x 11 1/8"	Plywood
2	Sides	1/2" x 4 1/2" x 11 1/8"	Alder
1	Back	1/2" x 4 1/2" x 10 1/8"	Alder
2	Fronts	1/2" x 4 1/2" x 3"	Alder
1	Lid	3/4" x 9" x 11"	Cherry
3	Dividers	1/4" x 9" x 12 1/2"	Masonite

Sandpaper Press

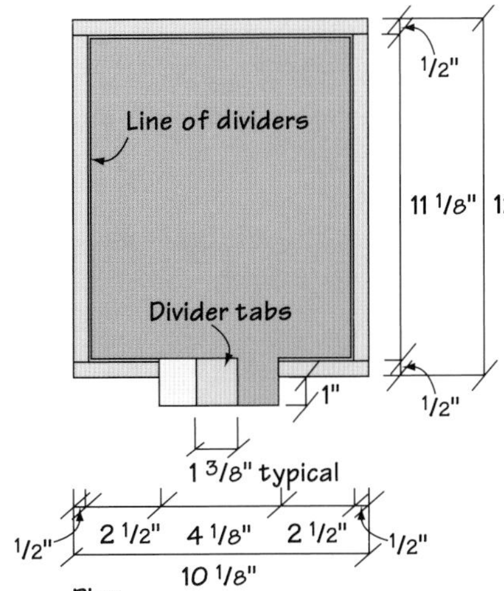

Line of dividers
Divider tabs
1/2"
11 1/8"
12 1/8"
1/2"
1"
1 3/8" typical
1/2"
2 1/2"
4 1/8"
2 1/2"
1/2"
10 1/8"

Plan

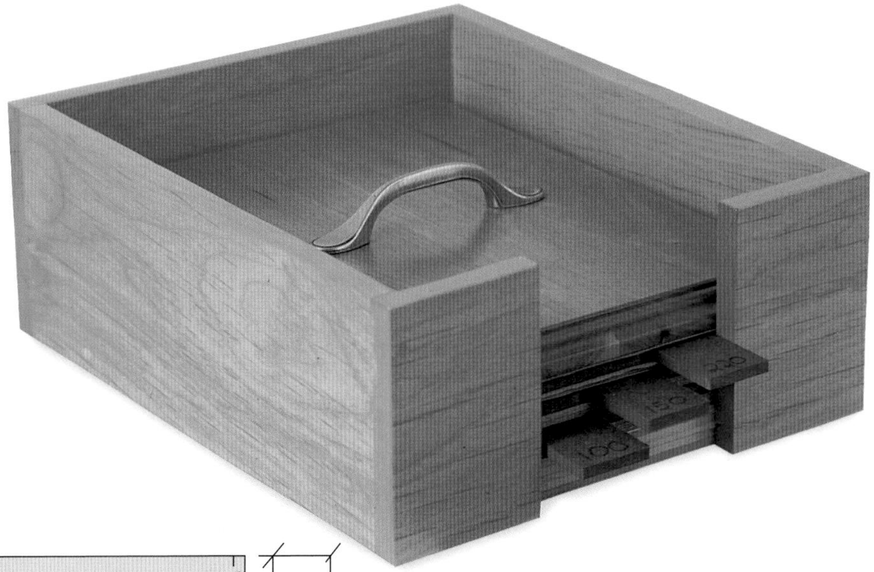

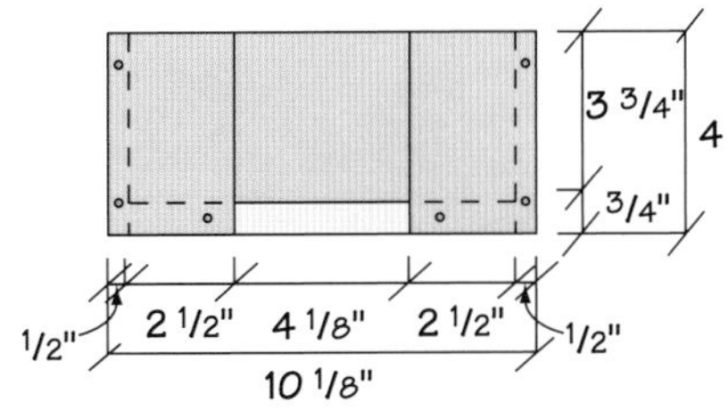

3 3/4"
4 1/2"
3/4"
1/2"
2 1/2"
4 1/8"
2 1/2"
1/2"
10 1/8"

Elevation

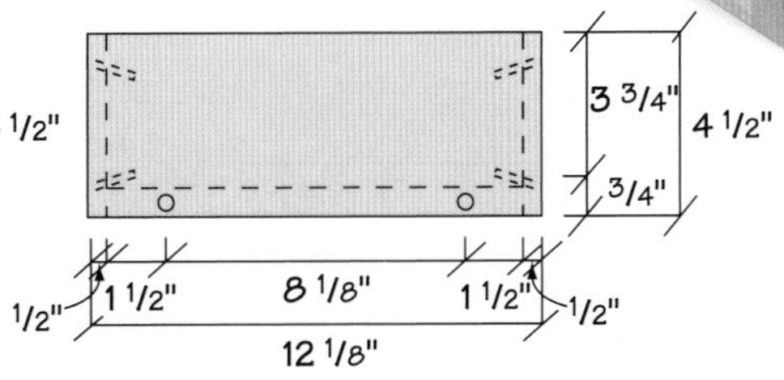

3 3/4"
4 1/2"
3/4"
1/2"
1 1/2"
8 1/8"
1 1/2"
1/2"
12 1/8"

Profile

Start construction by cutting the sides and ends as given in the schedule of materials, then cut the bottom. The joinery holding the box together can be as simple as screwed or nailed butt joints. If you're feeling frisky, try some hand-cut dovetails. I opted for the happy medium of pegged butt joints. By drilling the peg holes at opposing angles, you will get an especially strong joint.

Sand the interior faces of the sides, ends and bottom. Then glue and clamp the sides and ends in place around the bottom. Don't glue the bottom in place at this time; just use it as a guide. With a 3/16" bit, drill to a 1 1/4" depth about 3/4" from each corner, angling the bit toward the center. Now apply a small amount of glue to the tip of a 3/16"-diameter dowel (cut to about 1 1/2" long) and tap it into the hole. Repeat this process on the other three corners.

After the glue has set, remove the clamps and the bottom. Apply a small amount of glue to the edges of the bottom (except for the exposed front) and place it back within the box frame flush to the bottom. Clamp the sides to the bottom, then repeat the pegging process around the perimeter of the base. Use two pegs per side and back, and one per front piece. Once the glue is dry, cut the dowels flush to the surface of the sides and sand the outside of the box.

The lid is very simple and depends a great deal on your scrap pile. The one I used was cut from a small cherry door that was damaged. Use whatever material you like (including particleboard or plywood), as long as it has enough weight to keep the sandpaper pressed flat. The Masonite dividers are cut to fit within the box, each with a tab to extend through the front opening. The number of dividers depends on the variety of sandpaper used.

Find an extra handle lying around the shop and attach, then apply a quick coat of finish (optional). Now your curling days are over.

SHOP TIPS

STOP ON RED • As a strong visual reminder of where your fingers should never go, create warning areas near saw blades and router bits. For example, use bright red spray paint to create a warning zone a few inches all around your table saw blade. You can also use red electrical tape or red shelf liner (Contact brand) paper, replacing it periodically as it gets worn.

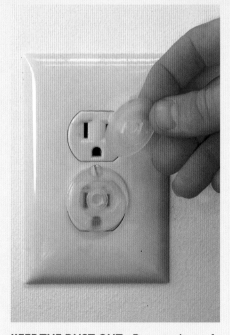

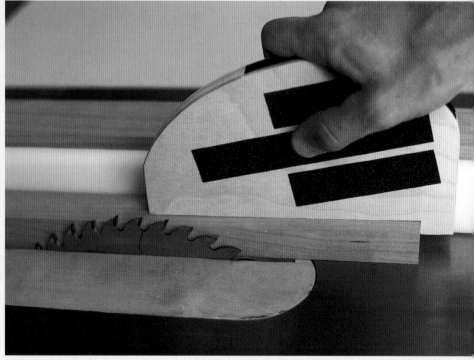

KEEP THE DUST OUT • Buy a package of the plastic outlet covers sold to keep outlets safe. Use the caps to seal unused outlets to keep dust and dirt from building up inside. Built-up dust in outlets is one common cause of workshop fires.

DON'T LOSE YOUR GRIP • Put non-slip tape (available at almost any hardware store) on push sticks, hold-downs, jigs and anywhere you want to make sure the wood or your fingers stays put while you're working. Non-slip tape is also a great safety feature for slippery workshop floors, ladder treads and steps. It's available in different widths and sometimes in colors, as well.

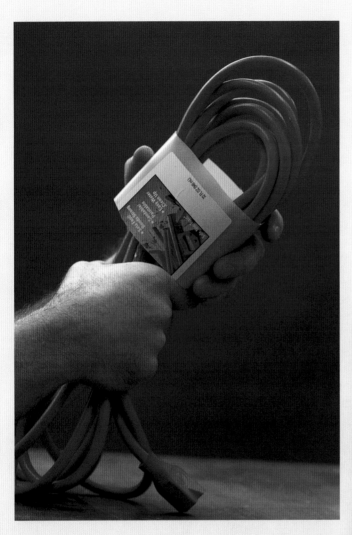

CORD CONTROL • Empty, plastic motor oil bottles can be cleaned and turned into convenient holders for tools or extension cords. Cut off the ends and slip the square middle section over a coiled cord. And, by the way, the spout end of the plastic bottle makes a handy little funnel.

FOAM STORAGE • Use a block of polystyrene foam ("Styrofoam") as a small tool holder. Buy a stable block of the stuff — put it on your workbench or use a hot-melt glue gun to mount it to the underside of a shelf. Little screwdrivers, hex-head keys, pens, awls and knives are candidates for residence.

TISSUE HANGER • It's great to have a box of facial tissues at hand when you're working, but how do you keep the box off your already-too-cluttered workbench? Bend a coat hanger into a square "U" and hang it from a hook — that's how.

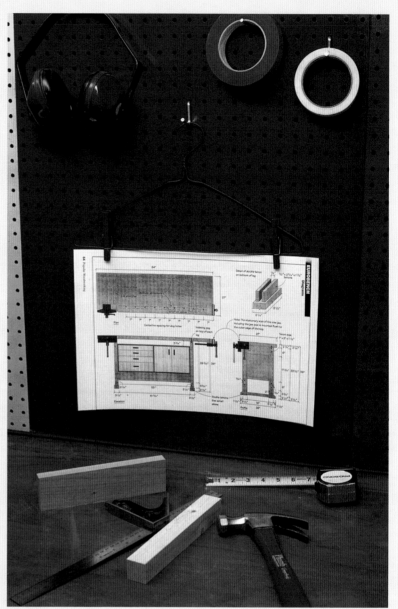

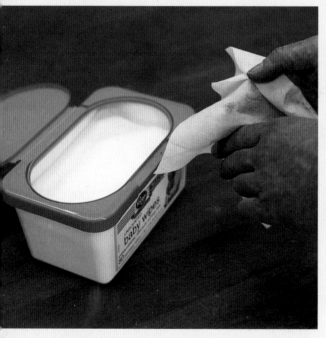

SIMPLE PLAN HOLDER • Use a pants or skirt clothes hanger — the kind with two spring-clips in the middle — to hold plans so you can see them. No more stooping over or ruining the plans because you forgot they were on the workbench top.

NOT JUST FOR BABIES • Keep a container of moist towelettes on your workbench for quick hand cleanups. The non-scented, generic store brands are cheap, but any brand will work. It beats the option of either frequent trips back into the house to clean your mitts or letting the grime build up.

PHONE-BOOK WORK SURFACE • Here's a new way to recycle old phone books. Keep one in your workshop to use as a work surface for small painting and gluing projects. When finished, just tear out the dirty pages and you'll have a fresh work surface next time.

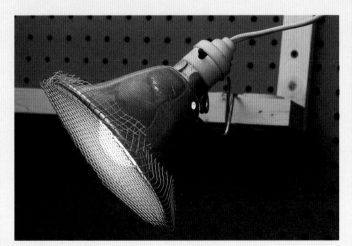

SAVE YOUR LIGHTS • Exposed light bulbs and tubes can't take much of a beating. Cut a piece of hardware cloth (a type of light wire screening) to fit over the light's end. It molds to fit, so it's easy to install and remove. Now your router can kick up a storm and you don't have to worry about suddenly being left in the dark.

SADDLE UP • Put this carpet saddle on your sawhorses to protect your projects from the horse itself. There are various ways to build this, but the elements are the same. Use some cheap, new carpet samples (old carpet will be too dirty) and a U-shaped bracket to fit over the sawhorse top. Or you can make this a permanent part of your sawhorse, replacing the carpet as it wears out.

Band Saw Master Jig

If you use the band saw merely for freehand sawing of curved components and an occasional resaw chore, you're selling short one of your shop's most versatile machines. Just adding an oversize table will improve your work. Add accessories to that table, and you can split cylinders or turnings, saw parallel curves, saw patterns, cut accurate circles and crosscut round stock. Tricked out, the band saw gains the status it deserves.

My master jig was designed for the average "small" machine. If your unit has a 12" to 14" cutting capacity from the blade to the post and your table measures about 12" to 14" square, you should be able to make it with a few alterations.

Before building this jig, check two things on your saw. With the trunnion at zero, make sure the angle between the saw blade and the table is 90 degrees. Also, verify that the saw blade and the miter-gauge slot are parallel.

by R.J. DeCristoforo
R.J. DeCristoforo was a contributing editor to *Popular Woodworking* magazine and, as a leading woodworking and tool authority, authored dozens of books.

The Table

Start With the Table

Cut a piece of cabinet-grade plywood for the jig's table to size for your saw, then use the table saw to form the $\frac{1}{8}$" kerf for the blade (see diagram). Next, form the T-slot for the pivot slide centered on the table. Cut the 1"-wide by 9" slot using your table saw to define the width of the slot (stop short of the final length). Extend the cuts with a handsaw. Remove the waste with a chisel. Now widen the bottom half of the slot to 2" with a dado or by repeated passes with a saw blade. The cuts make $\frac{3}{8}$"-deep by $\frac{1}{2}$"-wide rabbets (detail A).

Next, use your table saw to cut the slot for the miter gauge. Locate it 6" away from the outside edge of the table. Its depth and width must match the bar of your miter gauge.

Drill holes for the three $\frac{5}{16}$" threaded inserts as shown and install them through the bottom of the table until they are almost flush with the table's surface.

Table Guide

On the underside of the table, attach a table guide (B) that slides in the machine's miter slot. Here's how: Put the table guide in the saw's miter slot, then position the jig's table so its right edge and the guide are parallel. Secure the guide by tacking through the table, then attach the guide permanently with four no. 4×$\frac{3}{4}$" flathead screws from the bottom of the guide and glue. Drill shank and pilot holes for the screws so they won't split or spread the guide when installed.

Add the Braces

Prepare the part for the fence brace (F) and then cut the $\frac{1}{2}$"×$\frac{3}{4}$" rabbet. Attach the brace to the table with glue and 4d finishing nails. Now cut the table brace (C) to size and install the $\frac{1}{4}$" threaded insert as shown, then glue and clamp the brace in place until the glue sets.

Table Locks and Tie

Use an aluminum angle with 1$\frac{1}{4}$" legs for the table locks. Because some pivot-guided work requires good alignment between blade teeth and pivot point, a slot in the top leg of the angle is needed. This allows the jig's table to be moved to allow for blade width and tracking adjustment.

Drill holes through the vertical leg of the locks to match the holes that are in the table for adding aftermarket accessories. Use bolts to secure the locks to the saw's table and put the jig's table in place. Use an awl to pierce the underside of the table at the front end of the slot in the lock and then install the $\frac{5}{8}$" roundheaded screws.

Make the table tie from aluminum strap. Attach it to the underside of the table so it spans the kerf. The tie keeps the table level on both sides of the kerf.

Plan view of table

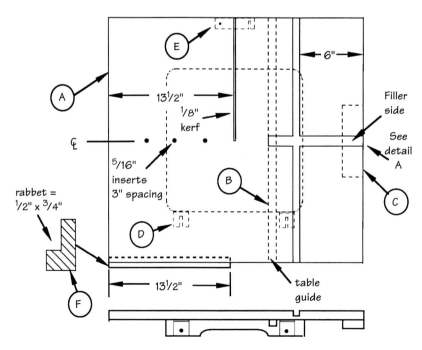

The Slides

The Pivot and Filler Slides

The filler slide (G) and pivot slide (H) have the same T-shaped cross-section and dimensions, so a good procedure is to start with parent stock that is 25" long and cut pieces to length after rabbeting the edges of the material. When the filler slide is in place, you'll see that it runs across the miter-gauge groove in the jig's table. So mark the location of the groove on the slide and then notch it so it won't interfere when using a miter gauge.

Mark the locations of the three no. 8-32 threaded inserts that are needed in the pivot slide. Install the inserts so they're flush with the top surface of the slide. Make the pivot points by removing the head from no. 8 screws. Chuck one of them in a drill press and form a point with a file, or grip the screw in a portable drill and spin it against a turning grinding wheel.

Detail A

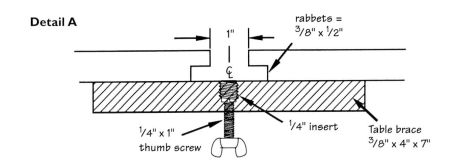

Table tie (Part E)

Table lock (Part D)

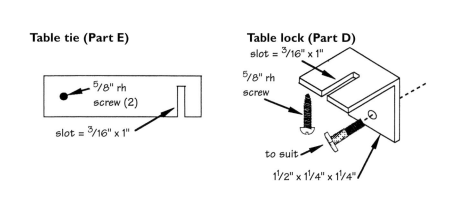

Pivot slide

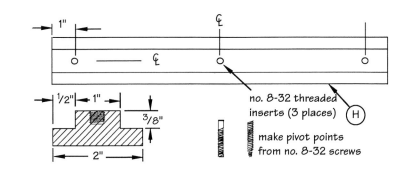

Filler slide

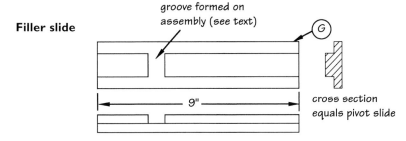

The Fence

Making the Fence

Cut stock for the fence body (I) to overall size. Shape the top edge on the band saw and smooth it with a drum sander. Next, cut the ends (J) to size and install the rear one with glue and four no. 10×3" flathead screws. Be sure to drill adequate shank and body holes and to countersink carefully before dri-

ving the screws. Before installing the front endpiece, carefully locate and drill the hole that is needed for the fence lock (K).

Now cut the fence lock to size, and accurately locate and drill the ¼" hole. Lay out the shape of the centered opening and saw away the waste with a band saw. Then use the band saw to

shape the lock's edge profile but don't try to shape the rounded end exactly at this point. Instead, work by hand with sandpaper to dress the end so that, when the lock is pivoted downward, the rounded end will bear firmly against the fence brace to secure the fence's position.

Parts of the fence

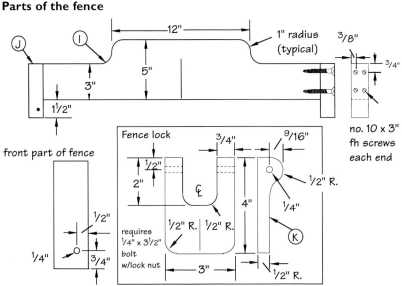

The V-blocks

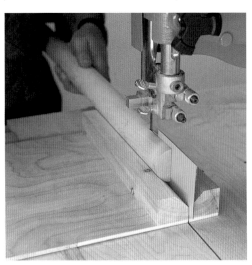

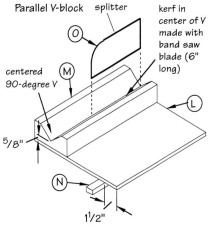

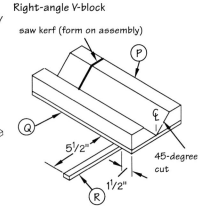

Accessories

Cut material for the V-blocks to size (M and P). Form the V-shaped trough by making a 45-degree bevel cut along one edge of stock that is 24" long and then halve the piece. For the parallel V-block, use glue and brads to attach the two pieces to the base so they form a V-shaped trough.

Prepare the base (L) and attach it to the bottom of the block with glue and brads. Size the guide (N) so it will fit snugly in the table's miter-gauge slot. A little on the snug side is good so the accessory won't move.

To set up the parallel V-block, put the guide in place in the table groove and position the block/base assembly so the cutting path of the saw blade will be on the center of the V-cut. Mark the position of the guide and attach it to the underside of the base using glue and brads. Place the accessory in position and, with a fine saw blade mounted, saw a kerf about 6" long.

Make the splitter (O) by rounding off the top forward edge and smoothing the edge. The splitter should fit tightly in the kerf. If not, cover the bottom edge with plastic tape to thicken it.

For the right-angle V-block, shape the guide (R) so it will ride smoothly in the table slot. Put the guide in the slot and position the V-assembly (P and Q) so the angle between its forward edge and the side of the saw is 90 degrees. Mark the position of the guide and then attach it to the block with glue and small nails.

Two Sawing Guides

Shape the front end of the guide (S and U) on the band saw and smooth the sawed edges with a drum sander. Drill a $5/16$" end hole for the slot and saw out the waste. The guide is secured to the jig's table with $5/16$" bolts that thread into the inserts installed in the table. The pattern-sawing guide is shaped like the one made for parallel curves except that the slot is shorter and the business end is notched to fit the saw blade that is used. The riser (T) is needed so the guide will be elevated above the workpiece.

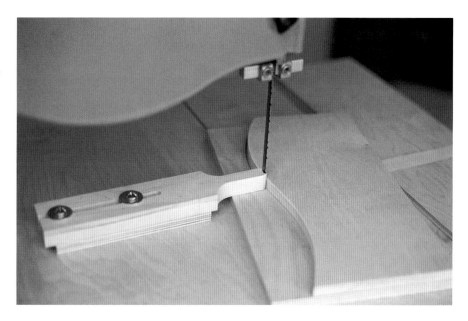

Pattern-sawing guide

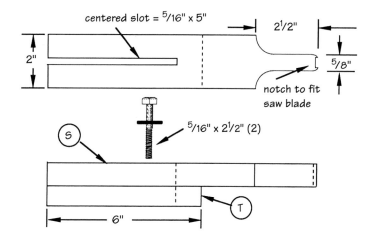

Parallel curves guide

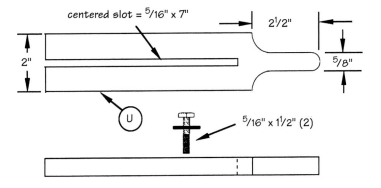

Dovetail Jig

Seems to me that most people think there are only two ways to cut half-blind dovetails: by hand or with a jig that can cost as much as $300. As someone who makes a lot of custom furniture, I can tell you that neither method has ever worked well for me. Sure, the size and spacing of hand-cut dovetails are easily customized, and it's nice to sometimes work in a quiet shop. But the handwork just takes too long when time is money. Dovetail jigs, on the other hand, are fast. But the size of your drawers is dictated by all but the most expensive jigs on the market.

That's why I've come up with a method that's fast enough to use in a professional furniture shop but allows you to space the tails almost any way

by Troy Sexton

Troy Sexton is a contributing editor to *Popular Woodworking* magazine.

you want. The price? Only $11 for a template guide and $8.99 for a carbide-tipped dovetail bit (you'd have to buy both for a dovetail jig, anyway). I've probably made more than 500 drawers using this method, and if you own a router, table saw and band saw, you can make them this way this weekend.

In a nutshell, here's how it works: While you're ripping your drawer pieces to width, rip an extra piece of scrap to use as a template. Use a dado stack in your table saw to cut notches on one end of the template — one notch for each tail. Clamp the template to the back side of your drawer front. Install the template guide and dovetail bit in your router, set the depth and run the router in and out of the notches. Congratulations. You've just cut the pins.

Now use the pins to lay out the tails on one drawer side. Cut the tails on your band saw. It's simple work. Occasionally you'll then have a little fitting to do, but after a little practice, your dovetails will fit snugly the first time.

Get Started

When you're doing this for the first time, keep in mind that all the measurements and settings I'm about to give you apply to drawers with $^3/_4$"-thick fronts and $^1/_2$"-thick sides. I use a $^{23}/_{32}$"-diameter template guide in my router (though $^{11}/_{16}$" or $^3/_4$" will work fine, as well) and a $^1/_2$"-diameter dovetail bit with sides that slope 14 degrees. See the supplies box at the end of the chapter for ordering information.

Begin by making the template. They're really easy to make. So easy, in

1 MAKE A TEMPLATE • A dado stack in your table saw is all you need to make the template for routing the pins. Don't worry too much about tear-out on the back side of the work. It's just a template.

2 VARIABLE NOTCH WIDTHS • When you finish making the template, here's what it should look like. For this 3"-wide drawer, I made two notches. Each of the teeth is ¼" wide. You can make the notches almost any width you want. The spacing can be varied by using a smaller template guide in your router.

fact, that I've got dozens of them for almost every size drawer I need. While you're ripping out your drawer parts, rip an extra piece of ⁵⁄₁₆"-thick stock for the template. Check the depth of your bushing because the thickness of your template needs to be slightly thicker than the depth of your bushing. For this particular drawer, my sides were 3" wide. Now go to your table saw and set up a dado stack. Don't worry about how wide the dado cut is; the idea here is to get a feel for how this system works. You'll see how to fine-tune the tails after you make a few templates. Set the height of the dado stack to ¹¹⁄₁₆". Now set your table saw's fence so there's ¼" of space between the fence and blade. Using your miter gauge and a piece of scrap attached to it, run the template on end as shown in the photo.

Turn the template around and run the other side of the template. Now move the fence away from the blade and remove more material from the template until you have three teeth on the template, each ¼" wide as shown in the photo.

Cut the Pins

Now set up your bench to cut the pins in the drawer front. Put the drawer front facedown on your bench. Line up the template on top of it and clamp the two together to your bench. Install the bushing in your router and then the dovetail bit. Set the bit's height to ¾" (including the bushing on the router's

Here, you can see how the bushing rides against the template, while the bit cuts the pins. When you cut your pins be sure to stand in front of the work so you can better see what you're doing. I stepped aside for the photo.

3 **PRECISION LAY OUT** • Now lay out the tails by tracing around the inside of your pins. A sharp pencil is key.

4 **BAND SAW CUTTING** • Cutting the tails on a band saw is a breeze once you get the hang of it.

Supplies

Bushings are available from many catalogs. Woodcraft, (800) 225-1153, carries several universal bushings that fit a wide range of routers:

1- Bushing - $7.50
1- Lock nut - $3.50

Carbide-tipped dovetail bits (1/2" diameter, 14-degree slope) are available from almost every woodworking catalog and home center. Expect to pay about $8.99 on the average, and a little more with specialty bit manufacturers.

5 **MULTIPLE TEMPLATES**
After a while you'll have enough templates to cut dovetails for almost any drawer.

template guide). Different depths will work. I use ¾" because the amount of carbide on my dovetail bit suits that depth perfectly. Cut the pins by running the router in and out of the notches.

Cut the Tails

The hard part is now done. Unclamp your drawer front and place it on top of its mating drawer side as shown in the photo. Using a sharp pencil, trace the outline of the tails onto the drawer

side. Cut the tails using your band saw or coping saw. Be sure to cut outside the lines for a tight-fitting joint. If necessary, pare the tails with a chisel. Then comes the moment of truth.

Let me say that after a couple attempts the truth won't hurt so much, so don't get discouraged. I think you can now see how easy it is to customize the location and size of your tails. Use a smaller-diameter bushing and you can make your tails even closer together.

This will require some trial and error on your part. Basically, the outside teeth will have to be slightly wider than ¼". And if you make different-size notches in your template, you'll produce drawers that are impossible to make with a $99 dovetail jig. Best of all, you can stop planning your projects around a jig, and you'll be cutting dovetails fast enough to have some hope of finishing your project when you actually thought you would.

Workmate Helpers

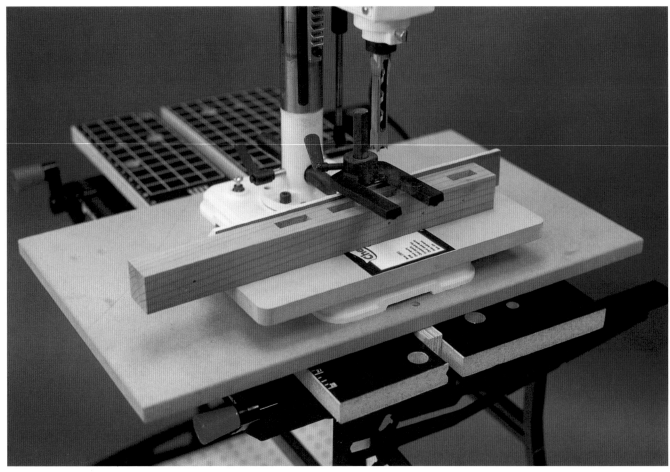

Is there any woodworker or home shop person who hasn't used a Workmate? The marvelous invention of British designer Ron Hickman, it combines a workbench, sawhorse and woodworking vise into a compact, fold-up portable package. We love 'em and so do you, as over 16 million Work-

mates have been sold since the first one came into existence in 1968. Not bad for a tool category that never existed before.

As good as Workmates are, you can make them even more useful with the following additions.

1 A PLACE FOR BENCHTOP TOOLS
If you had to pick one all-important, everybody-does-it use for a Workmate, its role as a stand for benchtop tools would probably be it. For all those tools you use only infrequently but need a sturdy, stable base when they are called upon, the Workmate provides an easy answer. Mount the benchtop tool to a piece of $3/4$" plywood, with a vertical "fin" on the bottom for the Workmate to clamp to.

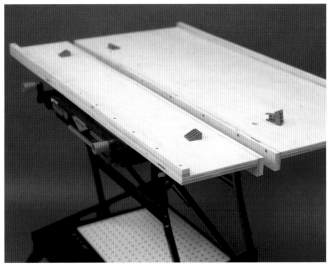

2 MORE WORK SPACE • As we all know, size does matter. The standard Workmate tops are a good compromise, but sometimes you just need more. You can easily build clamp-in-place work surfaces, as shown here, from ³⁄₄" plywood. We did two versions, one a large work area that doubled top space at the expense of being able to use the Workmate for any clamping chores, and a two-piece unit screwed to the Workmate top pieces to provide more clamping area. Because Workmates vary considerably in size and features, you'll have to tailor a bigger top to match your Workmate model. And, of course, don't make it so large that the Workmate becomes unstable.

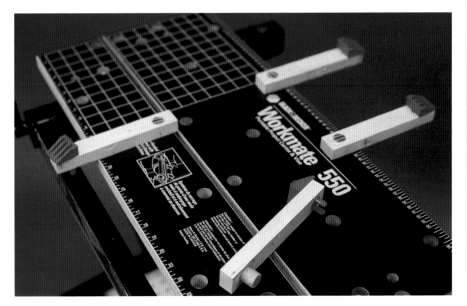

3 BIGGER BENCH DOGS • When you need bigger dogs or a wider clamping area than the Workmate offers, whip up this version in a few minutes with a piece of scrap and a ³⁄₄" dowel. Cut a piece of scrap to length — about 4" to 6" will do. Drill a ¹³⁄₁₆" hole in one end to accept the Workmate plastic bench dog and a ³⁄₄" hole in the other for the dowel. Cut the dowel so it extends about an inch or so from your scrap, then glue in place. When dry, it'll fit right into the Workmate's bench dog holes.

HOW THE WORKMATE WAS BORN

For an entertaining look into how the Workmate came to be and its British inventor, Ron Hickman, get ahold of a copy of *The Workbench Book*, by Scott Landis (Taunton, 1987). Chapter 16 is devoted to Hickman and his revolutionary design. The basic question is whether it's even possible to invent a new kind of workbench, which is what the Workmate is intended to be. We may think of it as more of a folding sawhorse, but it's much more than that, as Hickman demonstrates. The chapter where Landis interviews the inventor and recounts the 20-year development period from original idea to the first crude generation to worldwide recognition is a fun read. You'll find all the background information and photos of the early prototypes.

Tip *Has your Workmate been a loyal workshop companion — with the scars to prove it? Give your reliable old friend a new top. Use ³⁄₄" MDF or solid-core plywood, and use the old top piece(s) as a template. Drill new holes and reuse the hardware. You'll need a router and V-groove bit to cut grooves on the inside edge for clamping cylindrical items like pipe.*

Schedule of Materials • Circle-cutting Jig

No.	Item	Dimensions T W L	Material
1	Bottom plate	1/4" x 14" x 12"	Plywood
2	Top plates	1/2" x 5" x 12"	Plywood
1	Miter bar	3/8" x 3/4" x 15 1/2"	Oak
1	Slider bar	1/8" x 1" x 12 3/4"	Aluminum

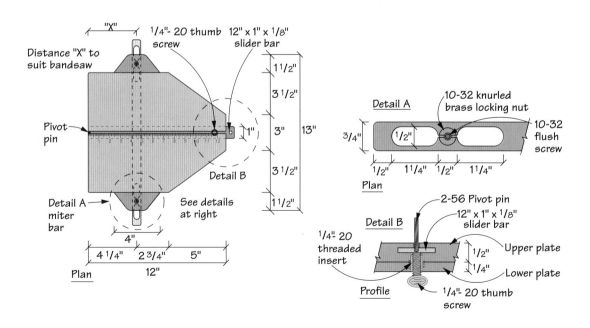

"X"

Distance "X" to suit bandsaw

1/4"- 20 thumb screw

12" x 1" x 1/8" slider bar

1 1/2"

3 1/2"

Pivot pin

3"

1"

13"

3 1/2"

Detail B

Detail A miter bar

1 1/2"

See details at right

4"

4 1/4"   2 3/4"   5"

12"

Plan

Detail A

10-32 knurled brass locking nut

10-32 flush screw

3/4"

1/2"

1/2"   1 1/4"   1/2"   1 1/4"

Plan

2-56 Pivot pin

12" x 1" x 1/8" slider bar

Detail B

1/4" 20 threaded insert

Upper plate

1/2"

1/4"

Lower plate

Profile

1/4" 20 thumb screw

Circle-cutting Jig

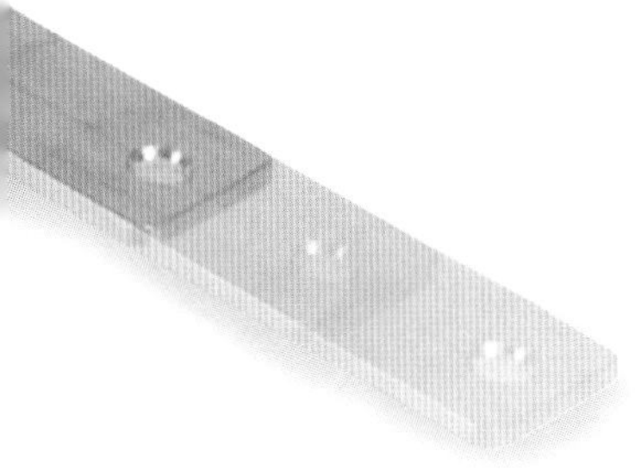

This jig allows you to cut circles up to 24" in diameter on your band saw and then clean them up on a disc sander. It uses an idea that's been around for decades, with a few refinements of my own.

Saw Work

First cut the pieces according to the sizes in the schedule of materials. The body is made of three pieces of plywood. The bottom plate is a piece of ¼" plywood, and the two top plates are ½" plywood. Cut a ⅛" groove in one edge of each of the top plates. These grooves will hold the sliding aluminum bar (see diagram detail). Then cut the corners off the top panels following the measurements in the diagram. Cut the bottom panel to the shape indicated in the diagram and glue it to the top panels, which should be glued along the edges you just grooved. When the glue is dry, cut another ⅛"-wide groove on the face of the panel that runs along the seam where the two top pieces of plywood meet. You should now be able to put the sliding aluminum bar into the groove and see it move through the panel.

Hardware

Drill and install a ¼" insert for the ¼" thumbscrew that will lock the sliding bar in place. Attach the screw pivot to the end of the sliding aluminum bar. I used a no. 2-56 machine screw inserted into the bar after tapping the bar using a tap and die set. After inserting the ¾"-long machine screw, cut off the head. Cut the miter bar to rough size and plane until it fits snugly but moves smoothly in your band saw's miter slot. The miter bar is locked into the miter slot with brass locking nuts on the top and screws that are flush on the bottom of the miter bar. Tightening the nuts compresses the miter bar vertically and expands it horizontally, locking it in place. Chain-drill holes on the miter bar in the locations shown in the diagram. Drill clearance holes for the locking nut and install the hardware. Attach the miter bar to the bottom of the jig using glue and screws. If desired, add a measuring gauge to your jig.

Put It To Use

To use the jig, place the device in your miter slot and set the aluminum bar for the radius you wish to cut. Lock the aluminum bar into place and then lock the jig into place on your table. Make a small hole in the center of the material you want to cut and place the material on the machine screw. Start the saw, pivot the material ... and your circle is cut.

by Angelo Varisco
Angelo Varisco is a woodworker in Woodbury, New York.

Table Saw
Troubleshooting

THE PROBLEM: *The saw doesn't make a square cut on the edges of boards.*

THE FIX:
- Raise the blade to full height and use a square to check that the blade is 90 degrees to the table. Adjust as needed and tighten the adjusting knob.

THE PROBLEM: *The boards bind between the fence and the blade or drift away from the fence.*

THE FIX:
- Check fence alignment. It should be parallel to the miter-gauge slot. Adjust the fence as needed.
- Saw blade may be dull. Replace if necessary.

THE PROBLEM: *When using the miter gauge, work binds and/or burns the edge of the board at the cut.*

THE FIX:
- Lay a carpenter's square against the miter gauge and blade. Slowly run the miter gauge in the slot and check the edge of the square against the blade. It should track parallel to the saw blade. Adjust miter gauge as needed.
- Measure front and back edges of the blade to the miter-gauge slot. The blade should be parallel to the slot. Adjust arbor or saw table per user's guide.

THE PROBLEM: *After a cut is made, rough saw marks are left on the edge of the board.*

THE FIX:
- Check alignment of the fence to the blade. Adjust until the blade is parallel to the fence.
- Replace dull blade if necessary.

Drill Press
Troubleshooting

THE PROBLEM: *The hole isn't circular.*
THE FIX:
- Check the runout on both the spindle and the chuck and adjust per owner's manual.
- The bit is bent or not chucked correctly.

THE PROBLEM: *Holes are not 90 degrees.*
THE FIX:
- The table isn't square to the bit and spindle. Check and adjust in several places, per the owner's manual.

THE PROBLEM: *Bits overheat.*
THE FIX:
- Sharpen or replace dull bit.
- Adjust the spindle speed per the tool's speed chart to match material.

THE PROBLEM: *Belts break too often.*
THE FIX:
- The pulleys aren't correctly aligned. Check and adjust.
- Belt tension is too high. Check and adjust tension every time the belt is replaced.

THE PROBLEM: *The chuck slips or slows down.*
THE FIX:
- The drive belt is worn or loose. Tighten or replace belt.
- Adjust speed per the tool's speed chart to match material.

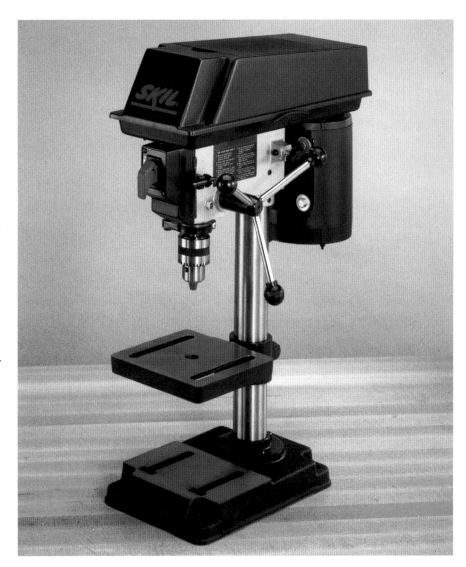

Shaper & Router
Troubleshooting

THE PROBLEM: *The work in the shaper or router kicked back.*

THE FIX:

- Always feed opposite the direction of cutter rotation.

THE PROBLEM: *Burn marks on wood cutter.*

THE FIX:

- Have cutters professionally sharpened or hone the flat side of each wing.
- Adjust the feed rate.

THE PROBLEM: *Work hits router table outfeed fence.*

THE FIX:

- Align the fence halves with a straightedge. Make sure that both pieces are 90 degrees to the table.

THE PROBLEM: *No support after the wood passes the router table cutter; snipe or gouge at the end of the cut.*

THE FIX:

- Adjust the outfeed fence to compensate when the entire edge of the stock is removed. Align the fence halves with a straightedge if only part of the stock edge is removed by the cutter.

THE PROBLEM: *The depth of cut is not uniform.*

THE FIX:

- Tighten down the router base properly.

THE PROBLEM: *Cuts are not smooth.*

THE FIX:

- Sharpen cutter properly.

THE PROBLEM: *Excessive chips accumulate between the fence and the work.*

THE FIX:

- Clear the exhaust port and check the vacuum system.

Band Saw
Troubleshooting

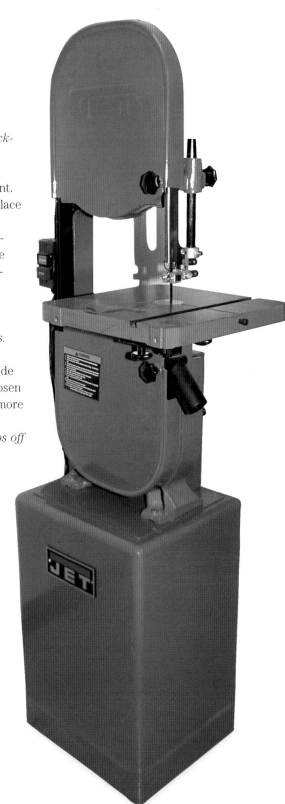

THE PROBLEM: *Blades break too often.*
THE FIX:

- Blade tension is too tight. Use the saw's tension guide and check the tension spring.
- The blade is too wide for the radius you're cutting. Refer to your owner's manual or blade manufacturer's guidelines for the correct width and tooth configuration.
- The saw may be clogged with dust and chips inside. Clean the saw every time you change the blade.

THE PROBLEM: *Blade won't follow the cut line.*
THE FIX:

- The guide is not properly adjusted. Adjust the guide blocks and thrust bearings according to your owner's manual.
- The blade is dull. Replace it.
- You're using the wrong blade (tooth configuration or width). Refer to your owner's manual or blade manufacturer's guidelines.

THE PROBLEM: *Cuts aren't square to the surface.*
THE FIX:

- The saw table isn't square (90 degrees) to the blade. Move the guide up and check the blade and table with a try square. Adjust.
- If the cut is bowed, either the blade is dull or the blade tension is incorrect. Tighten the blade per the tension scale.

THE PROBLEM: *Scraping or clicking noises.*
THE FIX:

- The blade has a kink or is bent. If you can't straighten it, replace the blade.
- The blade isn't tracking properly. Align the tracking to the center of the wheel, then adjust the roller bearing and guide blocks.

THE PROBLEM: *The blade binds.*
THE FIX:

- Binding is caused by side guide blocks that are too tight. Loosen and adjust them to provide more clearance.

THE PROBLEM: *The blade jumps off the track.*
THE FIX:

- The wheels aren't in-line. Check them and set blade tension and wheel angle.
- Back roller bearings are too far back. Adjust them to about $1/32$" behind the blade.

Sanders
Troubleshooting

THE PROBLEM: *The belt will not track on the stationary sander.*

THE FIX:

- Increase tension and adjust with tracking knob. Lock knobs into position.

THE PROBLEM: *The belt will not track on the portable sander.*

THE FIX:

- Check tensioning spring and adjust the tracking knob with the sander running.

THE PROBLEM: *Ridges appear in the sanded surface.*

THE FIX:

- For both stationary and portable belt sanders, check the platen under the belt for worn areas or chunks of material lodged in it. Remove foreign material or replace worn platen.

THE PROBLEM: *Burned areas on sanded surface or edges.*

THE FIX:

- On all belt sanders, disc sanders and spindle sanders: replace worn sandpaper.
- Use a lighter touch when sanding. Let the sandpaper do the work.

THE PROBLEM: *Sanded edges are not square.*

THE FIX:

- On all stationary sanders, square tables to the sandpaper and tighten adjusting knobs.

THE PROBLEM: *Paper comes off random-orbit sander while sanding.*

THE FIX:

- The sanding pad must be free from dust. Clean the pad and use a new sanding disc.

THE PROBLEM: *The sandpaper is worn only in certain spots.*

THE FIX:

- The sanding pad must be free from wood chips and have no holes in it. Replace if necessary.

THE PROBLEM: *The sandpaper comes off the pad sander while sanding.*

THE FIX:

- Spring clamps for holding paper need to be tight enough to hold the paper. Check and tighten or replace.

Jointer & Planer
Troubleshooting

THE PROBLEM: *Planed boards are not the same thickness edge to edge.*

THE FIX:
- Set table parallel with the cutter head per user's guide.
- Set knives parallel with the cutter head. Readjust with jig per user's guide.
- Adjust bed rollers parallel with the table.

THE PROBLEM: *Chatter marks appear on freshly planed boards.*

THE FIX:
- All knives need to be set at the same height in the cutter head.
- Take shallower passes.

THE PROBLEM: *Boards hesitate or stick in the planer.*

THE FIX:
- Wax the table or check bed roller height; adjust to .010" above bed.

THE PROBLEM: *Planed boards are sniped on the ends.*

THE FIX:
- Pressure bar tension may be too light. Check springs; replace if necessary.
- Bed rollers are set too high. Set to .010" above the bed.
- Check proper alignment of infeed and outfeed tables.

THE PROBLEM: *Jointed edges are not square.*

THE FIX:
- Square the fence and tighten the lock.
- Set knives to the same plane as the outfeed table.

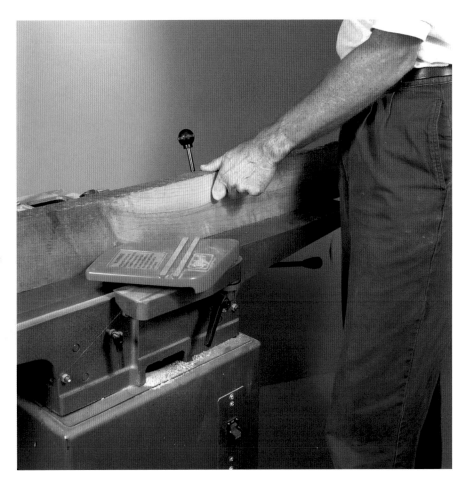

THE PROBLEM: *Work snipes at the end of the pass.*

THE FIX:
- Raise the outfeed table level with the knives.

THE PROBLEM: *Work hits the edge of the outfeed table.*

THE FIX:
- Lower the outfeed table to the level of the knives.

THE PROBLEM: *Rippled surface.*

THE FIX:
- Set all knives to the same height.

THE PROBLEM: *Jointed surface has ridges.*

THE FIX:
- Knives are chipped and can be offset to each other or replaced.

THE PROBLEM: *The cutter slows down or stalls.*

THE FIX:
- Check the belt for proper tension and tighten pulley if needed.

Power Hand Tool
Troubleshooting

THE PROBLEM: *The motor doesn't start or starts erratically.*

THE FIX:
- Replace the motor brushes (low-cost tools may not have replaceable brushes).
- Check the power cord for breaks.
- The switch is bad.

THE PROBLEM: *Circular saw doesn't cut at the correct angle or depth.*

THE FIX:
- The circular saw shoe is not locked tightly.

THE PROBLEM: *The drilled hole isn't round.*

THE FIX:
- Bent or dull bit, or too much pressure by the user.

THE PROBLEM: *Router work is kicked back.*

THE FIX:
- Always feed opposite the direction of the cutter's rotation.

THE PROBLEM: *Router leaves burn marks on wood.*

THE FIX:
- The bit is dull. Have bits professionally resharpened or replace them.
- Wrong feed direction or feed speed is too slow.

THE PROBLEM: *Router cuts are not smooth.*

THE FIX:
- The bit is dull. Have it resharpened.
- Wrong feed speed for material.

Index